ACHIEVE LEVEL

5

MATHEMATICS

Louise Moore
Series editor: **Richard Cooper**

Rising Stars UK Ltd., 22 Grafton Street, London W1S 4EX

www.risingstars-uk.com

All facts are correct at time of going to press.

First published 2002
This edition 2008

First edition written by: Richard Cooper
Educational consultant: Alison Toogood
Project management: Cambridge Publishing Management Ltd.
Project editor: Catherine Burch
Illustrations: Tim Oliver and Clive Wakfer
Design: Neil Adcock
Cover design: Burville-Riley Partnership

British Library Cataloguing in Publication Data
A CIP record for this book is available from the British Library.

ISBN 978-1-84680-288-1

Printed by Craft Print International Ltd, Singapore

Contents

How to use this book

What we have included:

★ Those topics at Level 4 that are trickiest to get right ('The tricky bits').

★ ALL Level 5 content so you know that you are covering all the topics that you need to understand in order to achieve Level 5.

★ We have also put in a selection of our favourite test techniques, tips for revision and some advice on what the National Tests are all about, as well as the answers so you can see how well you are getting on.

(1) **Introduction** – This section tells you what you need to do to get to Level 5. It picks out the key learning objective and explains it simply to you.

(2) **Self assessment** – Tick the face that best describes your understanding of this concept.

(3) **Question** – The question helps you to learn by doing. It is presented in a similar way to a National Test question and gives you a real example to work with.

(4) **Flow chart** – This shows you the steps to use when completing questions like this. Some of the advice appears on every flow chart (e.g. 'Read the question then read it again'). This is because this is the best way of getting good marks in the test.

(5) **Tip boxes** – These provide test hints and general tips on getting the best marks in the National Tests.

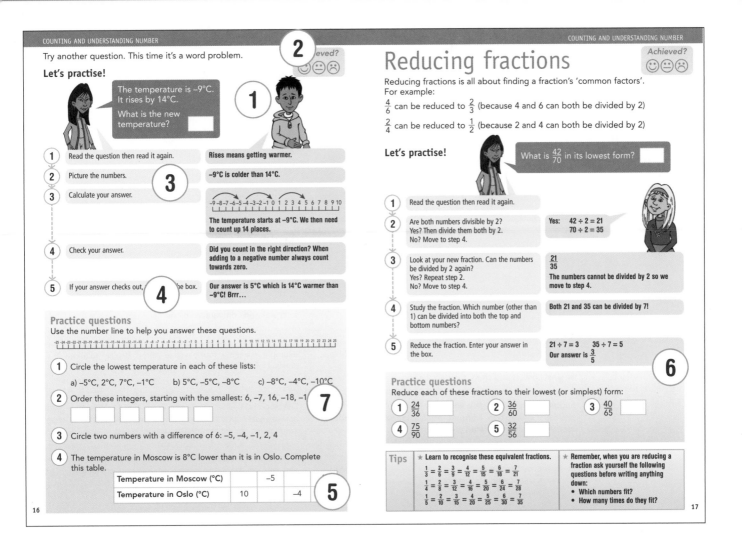

Try another question. This time it's a word problem.

Let's practise!

The temperature is –9°C. It rises by 14°C.

What is the new temperature?

1. Read the question then read it again.
   Rises means getting warmer.

2. Picture the numbers.
   –9°C is colder than 14°C.

3. Calculate your answer.
   The temperature starts at –9°C. We then need to count up 14 places.

4. Check your answer.
   Did you count in the right direction? When adding to a negative number always count towards zero.

5. If your answer checks out, the box.
   Our answer is 5°C which is 14°C warmer than –9°C! Brrr…

Practice questions
Use the number line to help you answer these questions.

1. Circle the lowest temperature in each of these lists:
   a) –5°C, 2°C, 7°C, –1°C   b) 5°C, –5°C, –8°C   c) –8°C, –4°C, –10°C

2. Order these integers, starting with the smallest: 6, –7, 16, –18, –1

3. Circle two numbers with a difference of 6: –5, –4, –1, 2, 4

4. The temperature in Moscow is 8°C lower than it is in Oslo. Complete this table.

Temperature in Moscow (°C)		–5
Temperature in Oslo (°C)	10	–4

16

Reducing fractions

Reducing fractions is all about finding a fraction's 'common factors'.
For example:

$\frac{4}{6}$ can be reduced to $\frac{2}{3}$ (because 4 and 6 can both be divided by 2)

$\frac{2}{4}$ can be reduced to $\frac{1}{2}$ (because 2 and 4 can both be divided by 2)

Let's practise!

What is $\frac{42}{70}$ in its lowest form?

1. Read the question then read it again.

2. Are both numbers divisible by 2?
   Yes? Then divide them both by 2.
   No? Move to step 4.
   Yes: $42 \div 2 = 21$
          $70 \div 2 = 35$

3. Look at your new fraction. Can the numbers be divided by 2 again?
   Yes? Repeat step 2.
   No? Move to step 4.
   $\frac{21}{35}$
   The numbers cannot be divided by 2 so we move to step 4.

4. Study the fraction. Which number (other than 1) can be divided into both the top and bottom numbers?
   Both 21 and 35 can be divided by 7!

5. Reduce the fraction. Enter your answer in the box.
   $21 \div 7 = 3$ $35 \div 7 = 5$
   Our answer is $\frac{3}{5}$

Practice questions
Reduce each of these fractions to their lowest (or simplest) form:

1. $\frac{24}{36}$ 2. $\frac{36}{60}$ 3. $\frac{40}{65}$

4. $\frac{75}{90}$ 5. $\frac{32}{56}$

Tips	★ Learn to recognise these equivalent fractions.	★ Remember, when you are reducing a fraction ask yourself the following questions before writing anything down:
	$\frac{1}{3} = \frac{2}{6} = \frac{3}{9} = \frac{4}{12} = \frac{5}{15} = \frac{6}{18} = \frac{7}{21}$	• Which numbers fit?
	$\frac{1}{4} = \frac{2}{8} = \frac{3}{12} = \frac{4}{16} = \frac{5}{20} = \frac{6}{24} = \frac{7}{28}$	• How many times do they fit?
	$\frac{1}{5} = \frac{2}{10} = \frac{3}{15} = \frac{4}{20} = \frac{5}{25} = \frac{6}{30} = \frac{7}{35}$	

17

6 Second question – On most pages there will be a second question. This will either look at a slightly different question type or give you another example to work through.

7 Practice questions – This is where you have to do the work! Try each question using the technique in the flow chart then check your answers at the back. Practising questions is the best way to help improve your understanding.

GOOD LUCK!

Learning objectives for primary mathematics

This chart allows you to see the progression from Year 6 to Year 7 for each strand following the New Primary Mathematics Framework.

The key objectives are in **bold type**.

Strand	Year 6	Year 7
Using and applying mathematics	Solve multi-step problems, and problems involving fractions, decimals and percentages; choose and use appropriate calculation strategies at each stage, including calculator use	Solve problems by breaking down complex calculations into simpler steps; choose and use operations and calculation strategies appropriate to the numbers and context; try alternative approaches to overcome difficulties; present, interpret and compare solutions
	Tabulate systematically the information in a problem or puzzle; identify and record the steps or calculations needed to solve it, using symbols where appropriate; interpret solutions in the original context and check their accuracy	Represent information or unknown numbers in a problem, for example in a table, formula or equation; explain solutions in the context of the problem
	Suggest, plan and develop lines of enquiry; collect, organise and represent information, interpret results and review methods; identify and answer related questions	Develop and evaluate lines of enquiry; identify, collect, organise and analyse relevant information; decide how best to represent conclusions and what further questions to ask
	Represent and interpret sequences, patterns and relationships involving numbers and shapes; suggest and test hypotheses; construct and use simple expressions and formulae in words then symbols (e.g. the cost of c pens at 15 pence each is 15c pence)	Generate sequences and describe the general term; use letters and symbols to represent unknown numbers or variables; represent simple relationships as graphs
	Explain reasoning and conclusions, using words, symbols or diagrams as appropriate	Explain and justify reasoning and conclusions, using notation, symbols and diagrams; find a counter-example to disprove a conjecture; use step-by-step deductions to solve problems involving shapes
Counting and understanding number	Find the difference between a positive and a negative integer, or two negative integers, in context	Compare and order integers and decimals in different contexts
	Use decimal notation for tenths, hundredths and thousandths; partition, round and order decimals with up to three places, and position them on the number line	Order a set of fractions by converting them to decimals
	Express a larger whole number as a fraction of a smaller one (e.g. recognise that 8 slices of a 5-slice pizza represents $\frac{8}{5}$ or $1\frac{3}{5}$ pizzas); simplify fractions by cancelling common factors; order a set of fractions by converting them to fractions with a common denominator	Recognise approximate proportions of a whole and use fractions and percentages to describe and compare them, for example when interpreting pie charts
	Express one quantity as a percentage of another (e.g. express £400 as a percentage of £1000); find equivalent percentages, decimals and fractions	**Use ratio notation, reduce a ratio to its simplest form and divide a quantity into two parts in a given ratio; solve simple problems involving ratio and direct proportion (e.g. identify the quantities needed to make a fruit drink by mixing water and juice in a given ratio)**
	Solve simple problems involving direct proportion by scaling quantities up or down	
Knowing and using number facts	**Use knowledge of place value and multiplication facts to 10 × 10 to derive related multiplication and division facts involving decimals (e.g. 0.8 × 7, 4.8 ÷ 6)**	Consolidate rapid recall of number facts, including multiplication facts to 10 × 10 and the associated division facts
	Use knowledge of multiplication facts to derive quickly squares of numbers to 12 × 12 and the corresponding squares of multiples of 10	Recognise the square roots of perfect squares to 12 × 12
	Recognise that prime numbers have only two factors and identify prime numbers less than 100; find the prime factors of two-digit numbers	Recognise and use multiples, factors, divisors, common factors, highest common factors and lowest common multiples in simple cases
	Use approximations, inverse operations and tests of divisibility to estimate and check results	**Make and justify estimates and approximations to calculations**

Strand	Year 6	Year 7
Calculating	Calculate mentally with integers and decimals: U.t ± U.t, TU × U, TU ÷ U, U.t × U, U.t ÷ U	Understand how the commutative, associative and distributive laws, and the relationships between operations, including inverse operations, can be used to calculate more efficiently; use the order of operations, including brackets
	Use efficient written methods to add and subtract integers and decimals, to multiply and divide integers and decimals by a one digit integer, and to multiply two-digit and three-digit integers by a two-digit integer	Consolidate and extend mental methods of calculation to include decimals, fractions and percentages
	Relate fractions to multiplication and division (e.g. 6 ÷ 2 = ½ of 6 = 6 × ½); express a quotient as a fraction or decimal (e.g. 67 ÷ 5 = 13.4 or ¹³²⁄₅); find fractions and percentages of whole-number quantities (e.g. ⅚ of 96, 65% of £260)	Use standard column procedures to add and subtract integers and decimals, and to multiply two-digit and three-digit integers by a one-digit or two-digit integer; extend division to dividing three-digit integers by a two-digit integer
	Use a calculator to solve problems involving multi-step calculations	Calculate percentage increases or decreases and fractions of quantities and measurements (integer answers)
		Use bracket keys and the memory of a calculator to carry out calculations with more than one step; use the square root key
Understanding shape	Describe, identify and visualise parallel and perpendicular edges or faces; use these properties to classify 2-D shapes and 3-D solids	Use correctly the vocabulary, notation and labelling conventions for lines, angles and shapes
	Make and draw shapes with increasing accuracy and apply knowledge of their properties	Extend knowledge of properties of triangles and quadrilaterals and use these to visualise and solve problems, explaining reasoning with diagrams
	Visualise and draw on grids of different types where a shape will be after reflection, after translation, or after rotation through 90° or 180° about its centre or one of its vertices	**Know the sum of angles on a straight line, in a triangle and at a point, and recognise vertically opposite angles**
	Use coordinates in the first quadrant to draw, locate and complete shapes that meet given properties	Use all four quadrants to find coordinates of points determined by geometric information
	Estimate angles, and use a protractor to measure and draw them, on their own and in shapes; calculate angles in a triangle or around a point	Identify all the symmetries of 2-D shapes; transform images using ICT
		Construct a triangle given two sides and the included angle
Measuring	**Select and use standard metric units of measure and convert between units using decimals to two places (e.g. change 2.75 litres to 2750 ml, or vice versa)**	Convert between related metric units using decimals to three places (e.g. convert 1375 mm to 1.375 m, or vice versa)
	Read and interpret scales on a range of measuring instruments, recognising that the measurement made is approximate and recording results to a required degree of accuracy; compare readings on different scales, for example when using different instruments	**Solve problems by measuring, estimating and calculating; measure and calculate using imperial units still in everyday use; know their approximate metric values**
	Calculate the perimeter and area of rectilinear shapes; estimate the area of an irregular shape by counting squares	Calculate the area of right-angled triangles given the lengths of the two perpendicular sides, and the volume and surface area of cubes and cuboids
Handling data	Describe and predict outcomes from data using the language of chance or likelihood	**Understand and use the probability scale from 0 to 1; find and justify probabilities based on equally likely outcomes in simple contexts**
	Solve problems by collecting, selecting, processing, presenting and interpreting data, using ICT where appropriate; draw conclusions and identify further questions to ask	Explore hypotheses by planning surveys or experiments to collect small sets of discrete or continuous data; select, process, present and interpret the data, using ICT where appropriate; identify ways to extend the survey or experiment
	Construct and interpret frequency tables, bar charts with grouped discrete data, and line graphs; interpret pie charts	Construct, interpret and compare graphs and diagrams that represent data, for example compare proportions in two pie charts that represent different totals
	Describe and interpret results and solutions to problems using the mode, range, median and mean	Write a short report of a statistical enquiry and illustrate with appropriate diagrams, graphs and charts, using ICT as appropriate; justify the choice of what is presented

Test techniques

Before a test

(1) When you revise, try revising a 'little and often' rather than in long sessions.

(2) Learn your multiplication facts up to 10×10 so that you can recall them instantly. These are your tools for performing your calculations.

(3) Revise with a friend. You can encourage and learn from each other.

(4) Get a good night's sleep the night before.

(5) Be prepared – bring your own pens and pencils and wear a watch to check the time as you go.

During a test

(1) Don't rush the first few questions. These tend to be quite straightforward, so don't make any silly mistakes.

(2) As you know by now, READ THE QUESTION THEN READ IT AGAIN.

(3) If you get stuck, don't linger on the same question – move on! You can come back to it later.

(4) Never leave a multiple choice question. Make an educated guess if you really can't work out the answer.

(5) Check to see how many marks a question is worth. Have you 'earned' those marks with your answer?

(6) Check your answers. You can use the inverse method or the rounding method. Does your answer look correct?

(7) Be aware of the time. After 20 minutes, check to see how far you have got.

(8) Try to leave a couple of minutes at the end to read through what you have written.

(9) Always show your method. You may get a mark for showing you have gone through the correct procedure even if your answer is wrong.

(10) Don't leave any questions unanswered. In the two minutes you have left yourself at the end, make an educated guess at the questions you really couldn't do.

Predicting sequences

Achieved?
☺ ☺ ☹

To achieve Level 4, you need to know how to predict sequences. This is not as difficult as it sounds. Sequences and patterns just can't live without each other!

Just remember: sequence = numbers following a pattern.

Pattern 1 The pattern may mean the difference between numbers is always the same:

2   4   6   8   10
   +2   +2   +2   +2

Pattern 2 The pattern may mean the difference between numbers changes according to a rule:

5   11   23   41   65
   +6   +12   +18   +24

Let's practise!

Predict the next two numbers in this sequence:

5, 18, 31, 44, ☐, ☐

(1) Read the question then read it again.

What is the pattern?

(2) Study the numbers.

What is the difference between the numbers?
5 + ? = 18   ? = 13
18 + ? = 31   ? = 13

(3) Test the pattern.

Is the difference between all the numbers 13?
      5   18   31   44   57   70
        +13   +13   +13   +13   +13

(4) Does the sequence work? If so, write in the next two numbers.

Yes, the pattern works and the next numbers in the sequence are 57 and 70.

Practice questions

Find the missing numbers in these sequences:

(1) 23, 35, 47, ☐, ☐

(2) 2, ☐, 12, ☐, 22

(3) 9, 5, ☐, ☐, –7

(4) 5, ☐, ☐, 23

Tips	★ You will see the pattern more easily if you write in the numbers underneath the sequence.	★ A sequence may be shown in pictures. Just turn the pictures into numbers to help you see the pattern.

	4 14 34 64
	   +10 +20 +30
		★ ★★ ★★ ★★★★
		           ★★ ★★★
		1 2 4 7
		  +1 +2 +3

Calculators

To achieve Level 4, you need to use a calculator correctly.
Used incorrectly, it can be a nightmare!

Let's practise!

There are a number of steps you can follow to succeed with calculators.

1 Read the question then read it again.

Does the question need a calculator? Can you work out the question in your head?

2 Press the keys carefully and methodically.

Think clearly. Talk through the calculation in your mind.

3 Check the calculator display.

Always check to see if you have pressed the right buttons.

4 Make sure you press the equals key (=) after each calculation.

Do not forget to do this!

5 Does your final answer look sensible? If not, go back to step 1.

If you feel the need to redo a calculation, don't hold back. A couple of seconds redoing a sum could save you a couple of marks!

Practice questions

Try these calculations on your calculator.

1 $345 \times 35 =$

2 $68.34 \times 59.8 =$

3 $586.3 + 275.95 =$

4 $606.6 - 60.06 =$

5 $503 \div 0.4 =$

6 $309 \div 0.03 =$

Tips	★ Don't forget to press the decimal point key when keying in decimal numbers. 3.5 = **3** **.** **5**	★ As you press each button, check to see what appears on the display.

Perimeter

To achieve Level 4, you need to be able to calculate perimeters. A common mistake is to miss one of the sides of the shape.

> The perimeter is the total distance around the outside of a shape.

Let's practise!

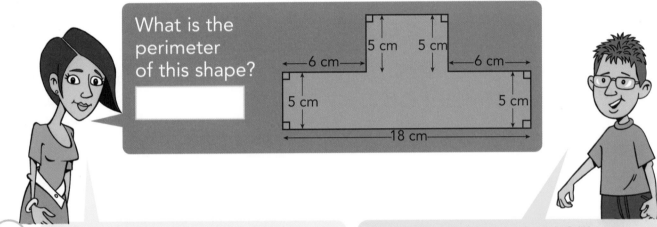

What is the perimeter of this shape?

1	Read the question then read it again.	What are we being asked to do? We are being asked to measure the distance around the shape.
2	Choose a side to start from. Put a line through it with your pencil.	This helps you to remember where you started from.
3	Add up all the lengths that are given in the question. Mark them off as you go.	5 cm + 6 cm + 5 cm + 18 cm + 5 cm + 6 cm + 5 cm = 50 cm
4	Now work out the lengths of the sides you haven't been given.	This is the IMPORTANT PART! The right angles show you that the distance along the top of the shape must be the same as the distance along the bottom. Both must be 18 cm. The missing side must be 6 cm because 6 cm + 6 cm + 6 cm = 18 cm.
5	Add the unknown length to the total of the lengths you have been given (see step 3).	50 cm + 6 cm = 56 cm
6	Is your answer a sensible one? If so, put it in the box.	The perimeter of the shape is 56 cm.

Tips	★ Think of a perimeter fence going all the way round a football pitch.	★ Don't try to measure 'missing' sides with a ruler. The reason they are missing is because the test wants to see if you can work it out from the given lengths.

The 24-hour clock

To achieve Level 4, you need to be a time expert. You should be pretty good at telling the time by now, but certain questions can still cause problems. It's very easy to make silly mistakes when working with the 24-hour clock.

Let's practise!

How long is it from 03:14 to 21:26?

1 Read the question then read it again.

2 Picture the question.

Imagine the times. 03:14 is very early in the morning; 21:26 is late evening. The answer will be quite high.

3 Count the minutes round to the first hour.

03:14 to 04:00 is 46 minutes.

4 Now count the hours round to the given hour.

04:00 around to 21:00 is 17 hours.

5 Add up the minutes and convert to hours if you need to.

46 minutes + the 26 minutes (from the time 21:26) is 72 minutes.
72 minutes = 1 hour and 12 minutes.

6 Calculate all the hours and add the remaining minutes to give a final answer.

17 hours + 1 hour + 12 minutes
= 18 hours and 12 minutes.

7 Does the answer look sensible? If so, put it in the box.

Yes, our answer looks sensible. 18 hours and 12 minutes is correct.

Practice questions

1 How long is it from 09:46 to 14:31?

2 How long is it from 15:48 to 23:15?

3 It takes Hannah 5 hours and 22 minutes to travel from home to London. If she sets off at 21:45, what time will she arrive?

Tips	★ Get used to reading timetables for buses, trains and aeroplanes. Test yourself on imaginary journeys.	★ Remember, when comparing times the fastest one is the shortest one.

Reading scales

To achieve Level 4, you have to use scales to measure things. They are just like number lines! The trick is to remember to work out what each mark stands for.

Let's practise!

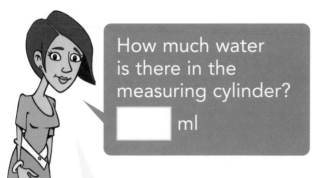

How much water is there in the measuring cylinder?

[ ] ml

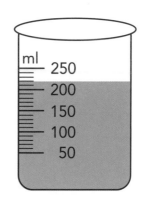

1 Read the question then read it again.

2 Picture the numbers.

The answer is between 200 ml and 250 ml.

3 Study the scale.

Count the gaps made by the small lines between 200 ml and 250 ml. There are 5 gaps. We therefore know that 5 gaps must equal 50 ml.

4 Calculate the scale.

5 gaps = 50 ml
1 gap = 10 ml (50 ÷ 5)

5 Answer the question.

Water level is at 200 ml plus 2 gaps
= 200 ml + 20 ml
= 220 ml

6 If your answer looks sensible, write it in the box.

If not, go back to step 2 and try again.

Practice questions

Which numbers are the arrows pointing to on these scales?

A [ ]   B [ ]   C [ ]

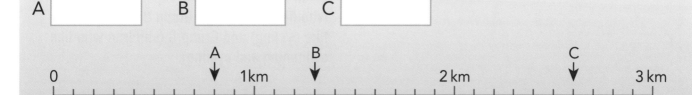

| Tips | ★ Read scales very carefully and count the gaps more than once to be sure you have got it right. Write in missing measurements in pencil to help you remember them. | ★ Always check your answer carefully to be sure it makes sense. |

Venn diagrams

To achieve Level 4, you need to be able to read all kinds of sorting diagrams.

Venn diagrams may sound complicated but really they are just a way of sorting information into groups. Look at the diagram. There are three regions – **A**, **B** and **C**.

Region **A** belongs to group A.

Region **B** belongs to group B.

Region **C** belongs to group A and group B.

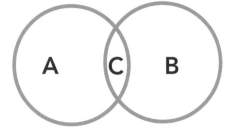

Let's practise!

Look at this table and sort the names into the Venn diagram. Decide on a description for each region.

Name	Likes swimming	Likes cycling
Ellie	✗	✔
Ryan	✔	✗
Junior	✔	✔
Abarna	✗	✔
Nirogini	✔	✗
Lisa	✔	✔
Alex	✗	✔

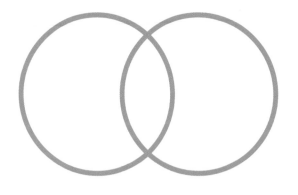

1 Read the question then read it again.

We need to sort the names into groups and decide on definitions or labels for each of these groups.

2 Study the information given.

We can sort the information we have been given into three main groups: Group A (children who like swimming), Group B (children who like cycling) and Group C (children who like swimming and cycling).

3 Sort the information.

Write out the groups on rough paper first.

4 Check your answer against your table.

Check back to make sure you have included all the children in the right groups before completing your answer.

Negative numbers

To achieve Level 5, you must understand negative numbers. Be positive! NEGATIVE NUMBERS ARE EASY. Imagine a thermometer with positive and negative numbers, and chill out!

Let's practise!

Put these temperatures in order from the coldest to the warmest:

11°C, 5°C, –5°C, –4°C, 2°C, –12°C, 15°C

(1) Read the question then read it again.

Negative numbers are colder than positive numbers.

(2) Picture the numbers.

Group the numbers.
Negative: (–5, –4, –12)
Positive: (11, 5, 2, 15)

(3) Study the numbers.

Draw a number line. Don't forget to include 'zero'. Decide where each number goes.

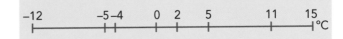

(4) Check your answer.

Are the numbers in order? Check you have used every number.

(5) If your answer looks sensible, write it in the box.

If not, go back to step 3 and try again.

| Tips | ★ **Numbers are often called INTEGERS. Don't let this put you off. This just means WHOLE numbers without decimals!** **These are integers: 1, 2, 3, 4** **These are not integers: 5.6, 7.8, 11.3** | ★ **When thinking of negative (–) numbers, think of a ladder going into a hole in the ground.** **–2 is higher than –6** **–2 is a larger number than –6** **–5 is below –4** **–5 is a smaller number than –4** 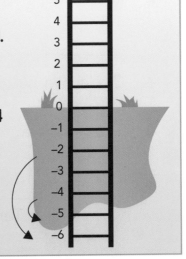 |

Try another question. This time it's a word problem.

Let's practise!

Achieved?

The temperature is –9°C. It rises by 14°C.

What is the new temperature?

1 Read the question then read it again.

Rises means getting warmer.

2 Picture the numbers.

–9°C is colder than 14°C.

3 Calculate your answer.

–9 –8 –7 –6 –5 –4 –3 –2 –1 0 1 2 3 4 5 6 7 8 9 10

The temperature starts at –9°C. We then need to count up 14 places.

4 Check your answer.

Did you count in the right direction? When adding to a negative number always count towards zero.

5 If your answer checks out, write it in the box.

Our answer is 5°C which is 14°C warmer than –9°C! Brrr...

Practice questions

Use the number line to help you answer these questions.

–25 –24 –23 –22 –21 –20 –19 –18 –17 –16 –15 –14 –13 –12 –11 –10 –9 –8 –7 –6 –5 –4 –3 –2 –1 0 1 2 3 4 5 6 7 8 9 10 11 12 13 14 15 16 17 18 19 20 21 22 23 24 25

1 Circle the lowest temperature in each of these lists:

a) –5°C, 2°C, 7°C, –1°C   b) 5°C, –5°C, –8°C   c) –8°C, –4°C, –10°C

2 Order these integers, starting with the smallest: 6, –7, 16, –18, –16, –20

☐ ☐ ☐ ☐ ☐ ☐

3 Circle two numbers with a difference of 6: –5, –4, –1, 2, 4

4 The temperature in Moscow is 8°C lower than it is in Oslo. Complete this table.

Temperature in Moscow (°C)		–5		0
Temperature in Oslo (°C)	10		–4	

Reducing fractions

Reducing fractions is all about finding a fraction's 'common factors'.
For example:

$\frac{4}{6}$ can be reduced to $\frac{2}{3}$ (because 4 and 6 can both be divided by 2)

$\frac{2}{4}$ can be reduced to $\frac{1}{2}$ (because 2 and 4 can both be divided by 2)

Let's practise!

What is $\frac{42}{70}$ in its lowest form?

1 Read the question then read it again.

2 Are both numbers divisible by 2?
Yes? Then divide them both by 2.
No? Move to step 4.

Yes: $42 \div 2 = 21$
         $70 \div 2 = 35$

3 Look at your new fraction. Can the numbers be divided by 2 again?
Yes? Repeat step 2.
No? Move to step 4.

$\frac{21}{35}$
The numbers cannot be divided by 2 so we move to step 4.

4 Study the fraction. Which number (other than 1) can be divided into both the top and bottom numbers?

Both 21 and 35 can be divided by 7!

5 Reduce the fraction. Enter your answer in the box.

$21 \div 7 = 3$ $35 \div 7 = 5$
Our answer is $\frac{3}{5}$

Practice questions
Reduce each of these fractions to their lowest (or simplest) form:

1 $\frac{24}{36}$

2 $\frac{36}{60}$

3 $\frac{40}{65}$

4 $\frac{75}{90}$

5 $\frac{32}{56}$

Tips	★ **Learn to recognise these equivalent fractions.**	★ **Remember, when you are reducing a fraction ask yourself the following questions before writing anything down:**
	$\frac{1}{3} = \frac{2}{6} = \frac{3}{9} = \frac{4}{12} = \frac{5}{15} = \frac{6}{18} = \frac{7}{21}$	
	$\frac{1}{4} = \frac{2}{8} = \frac{3}{12} = \frac{4}{16} = \frac{5}{20} = \frac{6}{24} = \frac{7}{28}$	• **Which numbers fit?**
	$\frac{1}{5} = \frac{2}{10} = \frac{3}{15} = \frac{4}{20} = \frac{5}{25} = \frac{6}{30} = \frac{7}{35}$	• **How many times do they fit?**

Ratio and proportion

To achieve Level 5, you need to use your ability to cancel fractions to simplify ratio and proportion statements.

Let's practise!

Have a look at this pattern of tiles:

What is the ratio of blue squares to white squares?

You need to find the ratio.

1	Read the question and read it again.	You need to find the ratio.
2	Count the blue and white squares.	There are 8 blue squares and 4 white squares.
3	What is the ratio of blue to white squares?	Blue:white is 8:4.
4	Can you reduce the ratio?	8 and 4 can both be divided by 4 so 8:4 = 2:1.

Now have a look at this pattern of tiles:

What is the proportion of blue squares?

1	Read the question and read it again.	Find the proportion of blue squares.
2	Count the blue and all the squares.	There are 8 blue squares and 12 squares altogether.
3	What is the proportion of blue squares?	8 squares out of 12 are blue, so the proportion is $\frac{8}{12}$ or 8 in 12.
4	Can you reduce the proportion?	8 and 12 can both be divided by 4 so $\frac{8}{12} = \frac{2}{3}$ or 2 in 3.

Equivalent fractions, decimals and percentages

You need to learn these facts to achieve Level 5. Working round this flow diagram can help make it easy!

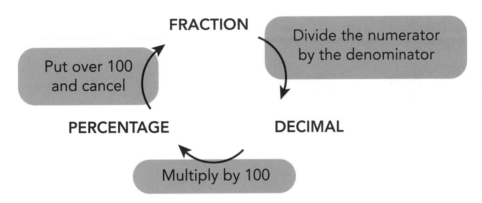

FRACTION

Divide the numerator by the denominator

Put over 100 and cancel

PERCENTAGE   **DECIMAL**

Multiply by 100

Let's practise!

Write $\frac{20}{32}$ as a decimal and a percentage.

1	Read the question and read it again.	We need to change a fraction to a decimal and a percentage.
2	Write the numbers.	$\frac{20}{32}$ reduces to $\frac{5}{8}$.
3	Change the fraction to a decimal.	Divide the numerator by the denominator, $5 \div 8 = 0.625$.
4	Now change the decimal to a percentage.	Multiply the decimal by 100. $0.625 \times 100 = 62.5\%$
5	Does your answer look sensible?	The percentage and decimal are both more than $\frac{1}{2}$. The answer looks correct.

Tip

★ Learn these common percentages, fractions and decimals.

$\frac{1}{2} = 0.5 = 50\%$ $\frac{1}{8} = 0.125 = 12.5\%$ $\frac{1}{3} = 0.33333333... = 33.33333...\%$

$\frac{1}{4} = 0.25 = 25\%$ $\frac{1}{10} = 0.1 = 10\%$ $\frac{2}{3} = 0.66666... = 66.6666...\%$

$\frac{3}{4} = 0.75 = 75\%$

Writing one number as a percentage of another

You can work out many fractions or percentages very easily without a calculator, but sometimes it's not so easy. For example, if you scored 15 out of 30 in your spelling test you should be able to recognise that you got 50% correct. If you improved the following week and got 24 out of 30 then you may need to use your calculator! Calculate as follows:

Key in

You should have the answer 80, which means you scored 80% correct.

To achieve Level 5, you need to be able to write one number as a percentage of another.

Let's practise!

Calculate 48 out of 120 as a percentage.

1 Read the question then read it again.

48 out of 120 means $\frac{48}{120}$.

2 Picture the numbers in your head.

48 out of 120 is less than a half, so our answer will be less than 50%.

3 Type in the numbers.

48 ÷ 120

4 Press the % key.

%

5 Does your answer look sensible? If so, put your answer in the box.

Our answer is 40%. It's worth taking a couple of seconds to check by redoing the calculation.

Practice questions

1 Use a calculator to express these fractions as percentages.

a) $\frac{117}{180}$ ☐   b) $\frac{286}{550}$ ☐   c) $\frac{81}{360}$ ☐

2 Express £560 as a percentage of £800. ☐

3 What percentage of 650 kg is 546 kg? ☐

Checking your answers

To achieve Level 5, you need to check your answers carefully!

Inverse operations

Remember, adding and subtracting are OPPOSITES. Multiplying and dividing are OPPOSITES. We can use this knowledge to check our calculations quickly.

> e.g. 75 + 85 = 160   CHECK   160 − 85 = 75
> or   42 × 6 = 252   CHECK   252 ÷ 6 = 42
> INVERSE means the same as OPPOSITE.

Let's practise!

5839 + 823 = ☐

1 Read the question then read it again.

5839 add 823

2 Study the numbers. Picture them in your head.

Picture them on a number line.

3 Perform the calculation.

```
    5839
  +  823
    6662
     1 1
```

4 Does the answer look sensible? If it does, check it using the INVERSE OPERATION.

The opposite of addition is subtraction, so ...

```
    5 1 5 1
    6662
  −  823
    5839
```

5 Does the check answer match the original sum? If it does, enter the answer in the box. If it doesn't, go back to step 1.

Yes! Our answer is correct!

Practice questions

Do these calculations and then check your answers using the inverse operation.

1 36 × 23 = ☐

2 6454 − 3759 = ☐

3 6453 + 786 = ☐

4 29,344 ÷ 56 = ☐

Tip	★ Get into the habit of checking your answers. It may help you do better in your test!

Rounding up or down

Another excellent way to check your answers is to round the numbers in the question up or down. Doing this will give you a simple sum to do and give you a rough answer.

Let's practise!

79 × 22 = ☐

1	Read the question then read it again.

79 × 22 = ?

2	Study the numbers. Picture them in your head.

Picture them on a number line.

3	Perform the calculation.

```
        79
  ×     22
       158
      1580
      1738
```

4	Now round off the numbers and mentally calculate your answer.

79 ROUND TO 80
22 ROUND TO 20
80 × 20 = 1600

5	Are the answers reasonably close? If so, enter your answer in the box. If not, you must go back to step 1.

Yes, 1738 is close to our estimate of 1600. It looks correct.

Practice questions

Do these calculations and then use the 'rounding up or down' technique to check your answers.

1 4763 + 7862 = ☐

2 47 × 64 = ☐

3 8675 – 749 = ☐

4 558 ÷ 31 = ☐

Tips	★ When rounding up or down think of 'friendly' numbers. These are numbers you can work with easily in your head. Some examples are 2, 5, 10, 50, 100 and so on.	★ Get used to doing mental calculations every day. Give your brain 'gym exercises' to do which involve calculating numbers quickly. Darts can be a fun way to do this!

Decimal numbers and tables

You should know your tables really well by now. To achieve Level 5, you should practise using your tables to multiply decimals. These are good mental maths questions – so no calculators!

Let's practise!

Write in the missing number.

$0.7 \times 0.08 = \boxed{}$

1 Read the question and read it again.

$0.7 \times 0.08 = ?$

2 Write the numbers.

0.7 is $\frac{7}{10}$ and 0.08 is $\frac{8}{100}$, so we are looking at very small numbers.

3 Multiply the digits in the question.

$7 \times 8 = 56$

4 Count the number of digits after the decimal points in the question.

0.7 has one digit after the decimal point and 0.08 has two – that's three altogether.

5 Write the answer with that number of digits after the decimal point.

0.056 has three digits after the decimal point.

6 Does your answer look sensible? If so, write it in the box.

0.056 is a very small number. Our answer looks OK.

Practice questions

1 $0.7 \times 6 = \boxed{}$

2 $0.8 \times 0.008 = \boxed{}$

3 $0.3 \times 0.8 = \boxed{}$

4 $0.6 \times 0.09 = \boxed{}$

5 $0.004 \times 9 = \boxed{}$

6 $0.05 \times 7 = \boxed{}$

Number properties

To achieve Level 5, you need to understand some important number properties.

Prime numbers

A prime number always has just **two** factors – itself and one.

The first prime numbers are 2, 3 and 5.

Can you find all the prime numbers up to 100?

Common multiples

Common multiples are multiples that are the same for different numbers.

The multiples of 3 are 3, 6, 9, 12, 15, 18 …

The multiples of 4 are 4, 8, 12, 16, 20 …

12 is a common multiple of 3 and 4 because it is on both lists.

Tests of divisibility

Divisibility tests are useful for checking calculations and explaining whether numbers belong in sequences.

A number can be divided by …	if …
2	it is even.
3	the sum of its digits is divisible by 3.
4	its last two digits are divisible by 4.
5	it ends in 5 or 0.
6	it is divisible by 2 and 3.
7	No 'ifs'. You have to work this one out the hard way!
8	half of the number can be divided by 4.
9	the sum of its digits is divisible by 9.
10	it ends in 0.

Using brackets

To achieve Level 5, you must be able to answer questions that contain brackets. This is not a problem – just remember this simple rule:

> **CALCULATIONS INSIDE BRACKETS MUST BE DONE FIRST.**

Look at this sum: $2 \times 3 + 4 = 10$

If we add brackets: $2 \times (3 + 4) = 2 \times 7 = 14$

Brackets change the answer!

Let's practise!

> Write in the missing number.
>
> $(52 - 29) \times 6 = \boxed{}$

1	Read the question then read it again.	$(52 - 29) \times 6 = ?$
2	Write the numbers. What do they look like?	**Rounding the numbers gives $(50 - 30) \times 6$.**
3	Study the numbers and think about them.	**$(50 - 30) \times 6 = 20 \times 6 = 120$**
4	Calculate the numbers in the brackets first.	**$52 - 29 = 23$**
5	Now complete the calculation.	**$(52 - 29) \times 6 = 23 \times 6 = 138$**
6	If your answer looks sensible, write it in the box.	**138 is close to our estimate of 120. Our answer looks right!**

Tip	★ Brackets are very sensitive and need your attention. **ALWAYS CALCULATE THE BRACKETS FIRST!**

Here is another question with brackets that we can do together. Try the practice questions at the bottom when you think you're ready.

Let's practise!

$$\frac{(34 \times 6) + (272 \times 3)}{30} = \boxed{}$$

1 Read the question then read it again.

What a long sum! What is it asking?

2 Picture the numbers. What do they look like?

Picture them on a number line. Is this a big number?

3 Calculate the numbers in the brackets first.

×	30	4
6	180	24

= 204

×	200	70	2
3	600	210	6

= 816

204 + 816 = 1020

4 Complete the calculation and then enter the answer.

1020 – 900 (30 × 30)
leaves 120
120 – 120 (4 × 30)
leaves 0
30 + 4 = 34

Practice questions

1 $3.2 \times (3.4 - 1.6) = \boxed{}$

2 $(57 + 135) \times 53 = \boxed{}$

3 $288 \div (92 - 56) = \boxed{}$

4 $(35 \times 42) + \boxed{} = 1800$

5 $\dfrac{(276 \div 12) + (500 - 388)}{5} = \boxed{}$

6 $\dfrac{(35 \times 15) \div (4^2 + 9)}{7} = \boxed{}$

Adding and subtracting decimals

To achieve Level 5, you need to work with decimal numbers. In addition and subtraction, working with decimals is easy if you remember to line up the decimals!

Let's practise!

Write in the missing number.

$78.53 + 6.85 + 925.2 = \boxed{}$

1	Read the question and read it again.	$78.53 + 6.85 + 925.2 = ?$
2	Write the numbers. What do they look like?	**78.53 is near 80; 6.85 is near 7. 925.2 is near 900.**
3	Study the numbers again and think about them.	**The answer will be around $80 + 7 + 900 = 987$**
4	Set out the sum, lining up the decimal points.	$\begin{array}{r} 78.53 \\ 6.85 \\ +\ 925.2 \\ \hline \end{array}$
5	Fill in any gaps with zeros.	$\begin{array}{r} 078.53 \\ 006.85 \\ +\ 925.20 \\ \hline \end{array}$
6	Complete the sum as normal, remembering the decimal point.	$\begin{array}{r} 078.53 \\ 006.85 \\ +\ 925.20 \\ \hline 1010.58 \\ \hline {\scriptstyle 1\ 2\ 1} \end{array}$
7	If your answer looks sensible, write it in the box.	**1010.58 is close to our estimate of 987.**

Practice questions

1 $45.65 - 7.8 = \boxed{}$

2 $384.1 - 76.42 = \boxed{}$

3 $74.58 + 26.8 = \boxed{}$

4 $68.423 + 7.87 = \boxed{}$

Tip	★ **The decimal points must be one on top of each other, including in the answer!**

Multiplying and dividing decimals

To achieve Level 5, you need to work with decimal numbers. When multiplying and dividing decimals, you have to know where the decimal point goes!

Let's practise!

Write in the missing number.

$4.45 \times 6.8 = \boxed{}$

1	Read the question then read it again.	$4.45 \times 6.8 = ?$
2	Picture the numbers. What do they look like?	It's nearly 4×7
3	Study the numbers again and think about them.	The answer will be more than 24 (4×6) and less than 35 (5×7).
4	Remember the rule!	Set out your calculation using the grid method. Don't worry about the decimal point yet.

×	400	40	5	
60	24000	2400	300	= 26700
8	3200	320	40	= +3560
				30260

5	Calculate.	Now put in the decimal point. Count three from the right. Your answer is 30.260 or 30.26!
6	Check your answer.	So, $4.45 \times 6.8 = 30.26$ 30.26 is just over 30.
7	If your answer looks sensible, write it in the box. If not, go back to step 3.	From step 3 we know our answer should be between 24 and 35. Great!

Practice questions

1. $8.43 \times 7.2 = \boxed{}$

2. $58.6 \div 0.4 = \boxed{}$

3. $24.2 \times 9.8 = \boxed{}$

4. $75.3 \times (34.2 + 5.9) = \boxed{}$

5. $56.4 \div 6 = \boxed{}$

6. $(29.4 - 8.72) \times 4.5 = \boxed{}$

| Tip | ★ When you multiply, there are the same number of digits after the decimal point in the question as there are in the answer! |

Long multiplication

Long multiplication is an important skill at Level 5.

Let's practise!

Write in the missing number.

578 × 32 = ☐

(1) Read the question and then read it again.

578 × 32 = ?

(2) Write the numbers.

578 rounds up to 600 and 32 rounds down to 30.

(3) Study the numbers and think about them.

578 × 32 is roughly 600 × 30, which is 18,000.

(4) To calculate the answer, first multiply by the units.

```
      578
    ×  32
     1156   (multiply by 2 first)
      11
```

(5) Next, multiply by the tens.

```
      578
    ×  32
     1156
    17340   (then multiply by 30)
      22
```

(6) Add your answers together.

```
      578
    ×  32
     1156
    17340
    18496   (then add your answers)
```

(7) Does the answer look sensible? If it does, write it in the box. If not, go back to step 3.

18,496 is close to the estimate. The answer looks correct!

Practice questions

(1) 375 × 53 = ☐   **(2)** 385 × 62 = ☐   **(3)** 396 × 37 = ☐

Tip	★ When you multiply by the tens, remember that your answer will end with at least one zero.

Long division

To achieve Level 5, you need to conquer long division.

Let's practise!

Write in the missing number.

987 ÷ 21 = ☐

1 Read the question and then read it again.

987 ÷ 21 = ?

2 Write the numbers. What do they look like?

987 rounds up to 1000 and 21 rounds down to 20.

3 Study the numbers and think about them.

987 ÷ 21 is approximately 1000 ÷ 20 = 50

4 To calculate the answer, start by working out the first part of the division.

$$\begin{array}{r} 4 \\ 21\overline{)987} \\ 84 \\ \hline 14 \end{array}$$

21s into 98 go 4. We subtract 4 × 21 from 98, leaving 14.

5 Bring down the next number and divide again.

$$\begin{array}{r} 47 \\ 21\overline{)987} \\ 84 \\ \hline 147 \\ 147 \\ \hline 0 \end{array}$$

21s into 147 go 7. We subtract 7 × 21 from 147, leaving 0.

6 If your answer looks sensible, write it in the box. If it doesn't, go back to step 2.

47 is very close to our estimate of 50, so it looks correct!

Practice questions

1 810 ÷ 18 = ☐   **2** 828 ÷ 23 = ☐   **3** 986 ÷ 34 = ☐

Tip	★ It helps to write out the table of the number you are dividing by – it's good for your mental maths too!

Fractions of amounts

To achieve Level 5, you need to be able to calculate fractions of amounts.

Let's practise!

Write in the missing number.

$\frac{5}{6}$ of 168 = ☐

1 Read the question and read it again.

$\frac{5}{6}$ of 168 = ?

2 Write the numbers.

$\frac{5}{6}$ is close to a whole, so the answer will be a bit less than 168.

3 Divide by the denominator.

The denominator is 6.
168 ÷ 6 = 28

4 Multiply the answer by the numerator.

The numerator is 5.
28 × 5 = 140

5 Does your answer look sensible? If so, write your answer in the box.

140 is a bit less than 168.
The answer looks correct!

Practice questions

Work out these questions **without** a calculator.

1 $\frac{5}{8}$ of 120 ☐

2 $\frac{2}{7}$ of 182 ☐

3 $\frac{5}{9}$ of 207 ☐

4 $\frac{11}{12}$ of 384 ☐

5 $\frac{3}{7}$ of 168 ☐

6 $\frac{7}{9}$ of 144 ☐

7 $\frac{10}{11}$ of 165 ☐

8 $\frac{4}{5}$ of 315 ☐

9 $\frac{8}{15}$ of 450 ☐

10 $\frac{6}{7}$ of 301 ☐

Calculating percentages of amounts

At Level 5, you need to be able to work out simple percentages with and without a calculator.

Without a calculator

Let's practise!

> A new mobile phone costs £170. In the sales the price is reduced by 15%. What is the new price of the mobile?

1 Read the question then read it again. What am I being asked to do?

Find the NEW price of the mobile.

2 To find the discount, first calculate 10% of the original price.

10% of £170 = £17

3 Now calculate 5% of the original price and add your answers together to find 15%.

5% is half of 10% so 5% is £8.50
(5%) + (10%) = (15%)
£8.50 + £17.00 = £25.50

4 Don't forget the next part! What is the NEW price of the mobile?

The mobile has been reduced by £25.50. So the new price is £170 − £25.50 = £144.50.

5 Check you have answered the question properly.

What is the new price of the mobile? After a discount of £25.50 the new price is £144.50.

With a calculator

You can also work percentages out using a calculator.

> Find 23% of 612

Let's practise!

1 Read the question and read it again.

23% of 612

2 Write the numbers.

This rounds to 20% of 600, which is 120.

3 Type in the numbers, then press the % key.

4 Does your answer look sensible? If so, write it in the box.

Our answer is 140.76, close to the estimate. Redo the calculation to check it.

Tip	★ To find 1%, find 10% by dividing by 10 and then find 10% of THAT answer. You can work out any % by adding all the 10%, 5% and 1% answers together!

Coordinates

To achieve Level 5 you should be familiar with coordinates and quadrants. Let's try a question to practise what we know!

Let's practise!

Write down the coordinates of each point on this graph.

1st quadrant = (__ , __)

2nd quadrant = (__ , __)

3rd quadrant = (__ , __)

4th quadrant = (__ , __)

Remember which quadrant is which!

2nd	1st
3rd	4th

(1) Read the question then read it again.

(2) Practise your answer.

You can sketch in lines to help you read the coordinates.

(3) Check the number of each quadrant.

2nd quadrant	y	1st quadrant
3rd quadrant		4th quadrant

(4) Read off the coordinates in each quadrant.

Remember, read:
ALONG the x axis first, then UP or DOWN the y axis.
1 (2, 3)   2 (–1, 3)
3 (–3, –1)   4 (1, –1)

(5) Double-check and write in your answer.

Check twice! Write once!

33

Using the y axis as a mirror line, draw a reflection of the pentagon in the 1st quadrant.

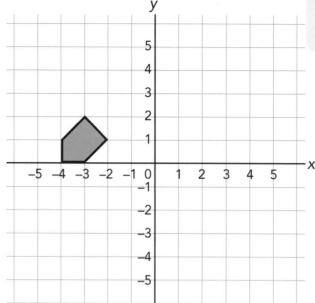

Write the new coordinates of each vertex here.

(__ , __)

(__ , __)

(__ , __)

(__ , __)

(__ , __)

1 Read the question then read it again.

Note you are being asked to work in the 1st quadrant. 'vertex = corner'.

2 Practise your answer.

Sketch your pentagon on rough paper first.

3 Note the position of your shape.

Your pentagon must go in the 1st quadrant, mirrored in the y axis!

4 Draw your shape on the grid above.

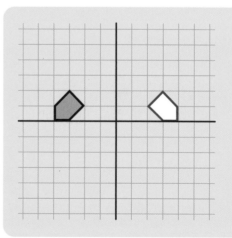

5 Read off your coordinates.

Remember, read along then UP/DOWN: (3, 0), (4, 0), (4, 1), (3, 2), (2, 1)

6 Double-check and write in the answer.

Check twice! Write once!

Symmetries of 2-D shapes

To achieve Level 5, you need to know how to reflect shapes in angled mirrors.

Let's practise!

Draw a reflection of this shape in the mirror line.

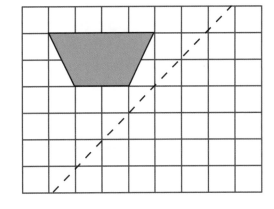

1 Read the question and read it again.

You need to reflect the shape.

2 Study the shape.

Trace the shape and mirror line on to tracing paper.

3 Position the reflection.

Turn the tracing paper over. Match the mirror line on the tracing paper to the mirror line in the question. Make sure the shape is now on the other side of the mirror line!

4 Draw the shape in its new position.

Draw over the shape on the tracing paper, then remove the tracing paper and draw the shape accurately with a ruler!

5 Is your answer sensible?

Check the answer using a mirror.

Does this shape have rotational symmetry?

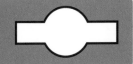

1 Read the question then read it again.

2 Practise your answer.

Trace the shape.

3 Test your answer.

Rotate the shape 360°. Does the shape look the same in any other position?

| 0° | 90° | 180° | 270° |

4 Check your answer and write it in.

Yes. The shape looks the same as it does at the start when it is turned around 180°! The shape has rotational symmetry of order 2.

Translating shapes

To achieve Level 5 in maths, you need to know how to translate shapes. Translating shapes is fun – just slide them across the paper. Make sure the shape stays EXACTLY the same though!

Let's practise!

Sketch the position of the shape after a translation of 3 squares right and 4 squares down.

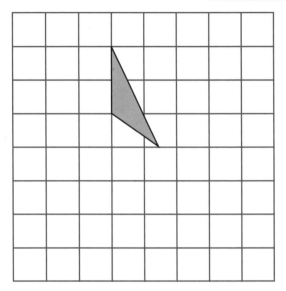

1 Read the question then read it again.

'translation' = slide along

2 Practise your answer.

Trace the shape and practise the translation before you write in your answer.

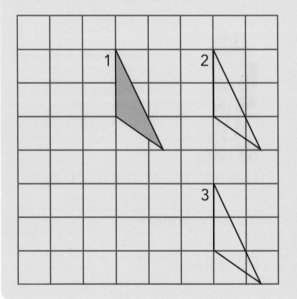

3 Draw in your final answer.

Double-check first.

Tips	★ Translate means 'slide along'. It is not the same as rotate, which means 'turn around'.	★ Check your answer by tracing the original shape and sliding the tracing paper over your answer. Does the shape match exactly?

Rotation about a point

To achieve Level 5, you need to be able to rotate shapes 90° or 180° about a point. It's easy – just turn the shape round.

Let's practise!

Rotate the triangle 90° anti-clockwise about point A.

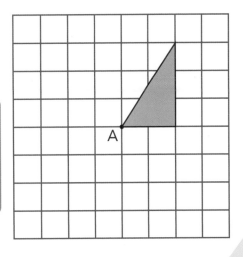

1 Read the question and read it again.

Rotate means turn.
We have to turn the triangle anti-clockwise one quarter turn.

2 Picture the shape.

Look at the horizontal and vertical sides and think where they will end up after turning.

3 Rotate the shape.

Trace the shape using tracing paper.
Keep the tracing paper in place and put your pencil on point A.
Turn the tracing paper 90° anti-clockwise.

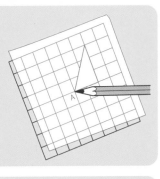

4 Draw the shape in its new position.

Check carefully where the vertices (corners) of the shape end up. If they were on a corner of a grid before, they should be on a corner now too!

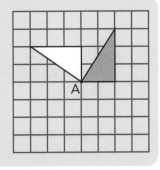

5 Is your answer sensible?

Check the question. We turned the shape 90° anti-clockwise. The sides on the new shape are exactly the same as on the original shape – the shape looks correct!

Tips	★ Remember – rotate just means turn.	★ DON'T turn your tracing paper over. You will draw a reflection of the shape if you do that!

Angles

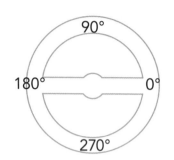

To achieve Level 5 you will need to be able to measure and draw angles and use the correct language for them.

Measuring angles

Use an angle measurer or a protractor to measure these angles.

a)

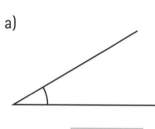

b)

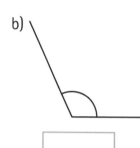

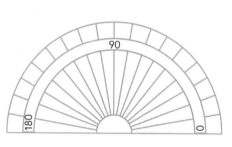

 1 Read the question then read it again.

2 Use the curved line to help you find the angle you need to measure.

Where will you measure? Use the curved line to help you.

3 Study the angles.

Estimate and label the angles to help you check your answers:
a) is an acute angle – less than 90°.
b) is an obtuse angle – more than 90° and less than 180°.

4 Measure the angles.

Match up the angle measurer and the lines carefully.

5 Check your answers against your estimates in step 3.

Does each answer match your estimate?

6 If your answer looks sensible, write it in the box.

If not, go back to step 3 and try again.

Drawing angles

Draw your first line (along the page). Then measure the angle you need.

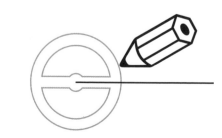

Draw your second line to join the first line at the correct angle you have marked.

Calculating angles

To achieve Level 5 you also need to be able to measure or work out the size of the angles in a triangle and at a point.

Just remember, angles in a triangle add up to 180°.

Let's practise!

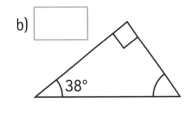

Find the unknown angles in these triangles.

a)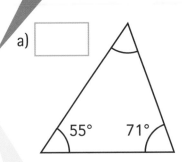

55°   71°

b)

38°

c) 51°

110°

1	Read the question then read it again.	We are given two angles. We need to work out the third angle.
2	Picture the shape and remember the formula.	Angles in a triangle add up to 180°.
3	Study the numbers.	You know two angles so you can work out the third.
4	Calculate your answer.	55° + 71° = 126° 180° − 126° = 54°
5	Check your answer.	Add the three angles together: 55° + 71° + 54° = 180°
6	If your answer checks out, write it in the box.	If not, return to step 3.

Can you work out the remaining two missing angles?

Tips	★ Always turn the paper to make the angles easier to measure. Keep your measurer straight! Make sure you read the correct scale. 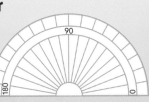	★ Think of a darts board to help you remember the angles in a triangle. One hundred and EIGHTYYYYY! 

Angles at a point

Let's practise!

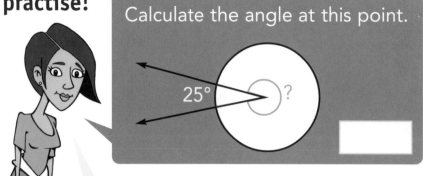

Calculate the angle at this point.

25° ?

1	Read the question then read it again.	'Calculate' usually means you need to do a sum to work out the answer!
2	Picture the shape. Estimate the angle.	The angle is between 180° and 360°.
3	Remember the formula.	A complete turn = 360°.
4	Study the numbers.	You know one angle so you can work out the other.
5	Calculate your answer.	360° − 25° = 335°
6	Check your answer.	Does it match your estimate?
7	If your answer checks out, write it in the box.	If not, return to step 4.

Practice questions

Calculate angle A in each of the questions.

1

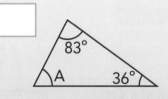

83° A 36°

2

124° A 86°

3

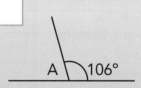

A 106°

4

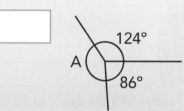

75° A

Units of measure

Comparing metric to imperial units of measure

To achieve Level 5 you will have to answer questions that ask you to compare metric units of measurement (kilometres, grams, litres and centimetres) with imperial units of measurement (miles, pounds, pints). Look at the conversions in the Key facts on page 62.

Let's practise!

Which is longer: 4 feet and 5 inches or 125 cm, and by how much?

1	Read the question and read it again.	**Find how many cm in 4 feet and 3 inches.**
2	Study the units.	**1 foot = 30 cm** **1 inch = 2.5 cm**
3	Convert the units.	**4 feet = 4 × 30 cm = 120 cm** **5 inches = 2.5 × 5 cm = 12.5 cm**
4	Add the units.	**4 feet 5 inches = 120 + 12.5 = 132.5 cm**
5	Answer the question.	**4 feet 5 inches is longer by** **132.5 − 125 = 7.5 cm**

Practice questions

1 Cameron drinks 9 pints of milk a week. How many litres is that?

2 Safi's dog weighs 20 lbs. How many kilograms does it weigh?

Tip	★ **Revision rhymes!** *A metre is just 3 feet 3. It's longer than a yard you see!* *2 and a bit pounds of jam is round about 1 kilo of ham!*

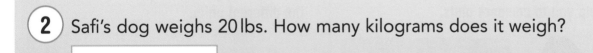

Converting metric units of measure

To achieve Level 5, you will have to answer questions that ask you to convert one metric unit to another metric unit.

Let's practise!

Write 6.51 kg as grams.

1 Read the question, then read it again.

6.51 kg = _____ g

2 Study the units.

1 kg = 1000 g

3 Calculate the answer.

6.51 × 1000 = 6510

4 Add in the correct units.

6510 g

5 If your answer looks sensible, write it in the box.

If not, go back to step 2.

Practice questions

1 A tank holds 50 litres of water. How many millilitres is that?

2 Convert 78.43 m to centimetres.

3 How many kilograms are there in 46,752 g?

Tips	★ Make up some of your own questions to help you to compare units.	★ Measure things around you to get a feel for the different units.

What would you prefer, 1 litre or 1000 ml of cola?

mm or cm

or

m

The area of a rectangle

To achieve Level 5, you need to work out the area of a rectangle.
It's easy – just remember this formula:

the area of a rectangle = the length × the width

Let's practise!

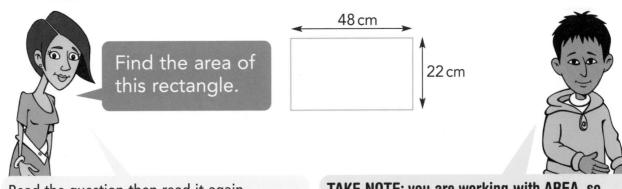

Find the area of this rectangle.

48 cm

22 cm

1	Read the question then read it again.	**TAKE NOTE: you are working with AREA, so you need a formula!**
2	Remember your formula.	**The area of a rectangle = the length × the width.**
3	Picture the numbers. What do they look like?	**22 cm can be rounded down to 20 cm and 48 cm is nearly 50 cm.**
4	Study the numbers again and think about them.	**We can estimate the answer to be around 1000. (20 × 50 = 1000)**
5	Calculate your answer.	

×	20	2
40	800	80
8	160	16

$$= \quad 880$$
$$= +176$$
$$\overline{\quad 1056}$$

6	Add in your unit of measurement.	**cm squared (cm^2) = 1056 cm^2**
7	Check your answer against your estimate in step 4.	**1056 is close to 1000.**
8	If your answer looks sensible, write it in the box.	**If not, go back to step 3 and try again.**

Tips	★ When dealing with area, make sure the units are ALWAYS squared. e.g. cm^2 m^2 km^2	★ Break up complicated shapes into smaller rectangles to make the question easier to answer. Remember to add up the areas of all the rectangles to get your answer!

Let's try another question. Here is a shape you will have to divide up into smaller shapes.

Achieved?

Find the area of this shape.

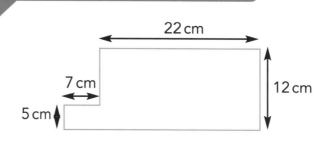

22 cm

7 cm

5 cm

12 cm

1 Read the question then read it again.

Look for the key words: area and shape.

2 Picture the shape.

It looks like two rectangles joined together!

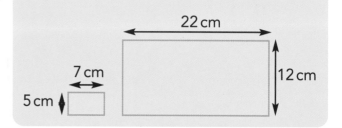

22 cm

7 cm

5 cm

12 cm

3 Remember the formula.

The area of a rectangle = the length × the width. We need to measure two rectangles.

4 Find the areas of the two rectangles. Then add them together.

$22 \times 12 = 264$
$7 \times 5 = 35$
Total = 299

5 Add in your unit of measurement.

$299 \, cm^2$

6 If your answer looks sensible, write it in the box.

If not, go back to step 2 and try again.

Practice questions

Try some more questions. If you need to find a missing length, look back at page 11.

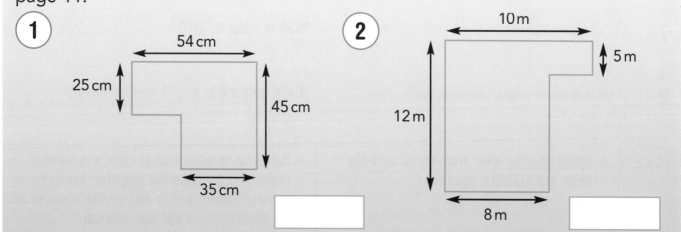

1

54 cm

25 cm

45 cm

35 cm

2

10 m

5 m

12 m

8 m

Finding the mean and median

To achieve Level 5, you need to know how to work out the mean and median of sets of numbers.

To find the mean, all you have to do is add all the amounts and divide the answer by the number of amounts. For example:

2, 2, 4, 6, 10, 12

The mean = (2 + 2 + 4 + 6 + 10 + 12) ÷ 6

36 ÷ 6 = 6

The median is the **middle number** in a group of numbers. To find the median, put the numbers in order from smallest to largest and find the middle number. For example:

48, 23, 67, 94, 12, 73, 88

order is 12, 23, 48, 67, 73, 88, 94

median = 67 (the middle number)

Practice questions

1 Find the mean of these sets of numbers:

a) 3, 7, 13, 8, 5, 6 [   ]

b) 35, 86, 64, 69, 21 [   ]

c) 345, 874, 65, 364 [   ]

d) 573, 100, 876, 52, 138, 97 [   ]

2 Find the median of these sets of numbers:

a) 4, 7, 8, 4, 6, 3, 6 [   ]

b) 5, 8, 4, 8, 8, 5, 2, 1, 5, 9, 0 [   ]

c) 54, 57, 56, 75, 65, 46, 57, 45, 65, 67, 45 [   ]

Tips	★ Remember: the mean is the same as 'average'.	★ To help you remember what the median is, think small, *medium*, large. (Median is in the middle!)

Comparing two data sets

Achieved? 😊 😐 ☹

To achieve Level 5, you should be able to compare two sets of data using the mean, median, mode and range.

Let's practise!

These are the marks Sam and Kani got in their maths tests. Each test was out of 25.

Sam	23	20	16	22	12	21
Kani	19	24	18	21	20	24

Use the range and mean to work out who has the better results.

1 Read the question and read it again.

Compare the range and mean.

2 Think about the numbers.

They both had weeks when they did better than the other.

3 Calculate the ranges.

Sam: 23 – 12 = 11
Kani: 24 – 18 = 6

4 Calculate the means.

Sam: (23 + 20 + 16 + 22 + 12 + 21) ÷ 6 = 19
Kani: (19 + 24 + 18 + 21 + 20 + 24) ÷ 6 = 21

5 Compare the results.

Sam: range of 11 and a mean of 19
Kani: range of 6 and a mean of 21

6 What do the results mean?

Kani had a higher mean, so her average mark was higher than Sam's. Sam had a higher range than Kani, so his marks were not consistent. Some were very good and some were bad! This means that Kani's results were better.

7 Does your answer look sensible?

Look back at the data. Kani always got good marks. The answer looks correct.

Conversion graphs

To get a Level 5 you will need to look at graphs like the one below and answer questions about them.

Let's practise!

These road signs are in miles. Use the conversion graph to rewrite the road signs in kilometres.

Graph: miles (y-axis, 0 to 50) against kilometres (km) (x-axis, 0 to 100)

Exeter 40 miles

Exeter [ ] km

Torquay 25 miles

Torquay [ ] km

Newton Abbot 15 miles

Newton Abbot [ ] km

1 Read the question then read it again.

Conversion graph tells us that we need to convert values.

2 Be methodical.

Exeter
- We need to change 40 miles into kilometres.
- Go up the *y* axis (miles) and find 40.
- Mark this point on the *y* axis with your pencil.
- Go across to the conversion line and make another mark.
- Now go down to find out the value in kilometres.

Our answer is nearly halfway between 60 and 70, so we can estimate 64 km! Now repeat for Torquay and Newton Abbot.

3 Does the answer look sensible? If so, fill in the answer box.

Check your answers carefully on the graph before writing them in the boxes. The test marker is looking for an EXACT answer.

Practice question

The exchange rate for pounds to stars is £1 = ★1.6. Using the graph above to help you, draw a new graph to convert pounds to stars. Use the graph to find out how much you would receive when you exchange:

a) £55 = ★ [ ]

b) £40 = ★ [ ]

Pie charts

Pie charts are an important part of Level 5.

Pie charts are a way of showing ideas as a fraction, percentage or proportion. They are an excellent way of showing information quickly and clearly ... as long as you know what to look for! Get used to seeing what the slices 'look like' so you can instantly recognise the proportions of a whole. It is worth drawing circles and practising dividing them into equal $\frac{1}{3}$, $\frac{1}{2}$, $\frac{1}{5}$, etc.

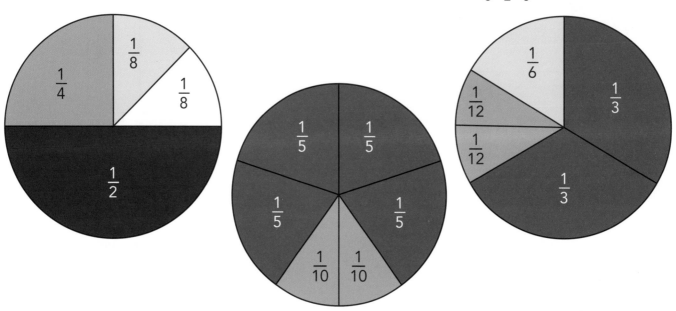

Practice questions

Use the pie charts above to estimate what fraction of the population of Birmingham is:

a) over 75

b) under 40

c) under 21

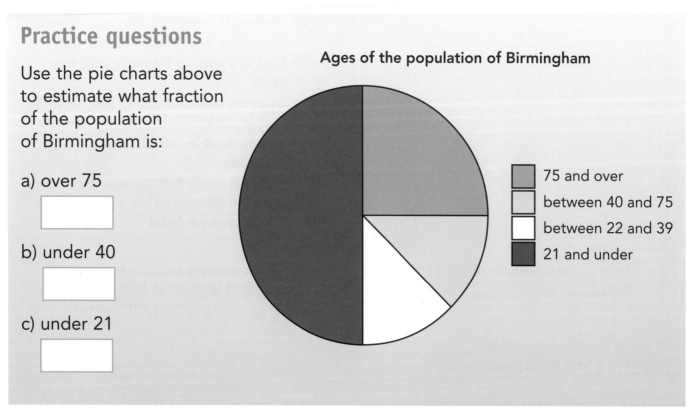

Ages of the population of Birmingham

75 and over

between 40 and 75

between 22 and 39

21 and under

| Tips | ★ Be **VERY** careful when reading scales or axes. You may be asked to find values **BETWEEN** lines on the scale. A test marker would want to know if you can find the **EXACT** answer. | ★ Always draw graphs and read graphs carefully and accurately. A sharp pencil, straight ruler and steady hand are essential! |

Probability

To achieve Level 5, you need to understand probability.

The probability scale is a way of showing how likely something is to happen on a scale of 0 to 1.

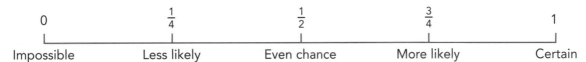

Here are some examples:

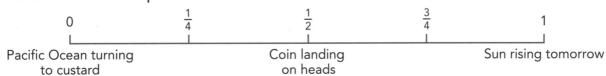

You will have to answer two types of question about probability scales.

Let's practise!

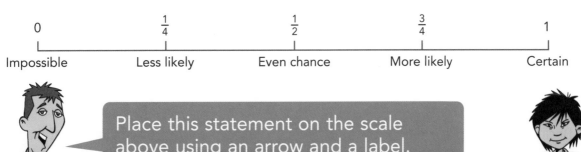

1 Read the question then read it again.		**Important here as there are more words than numbers!**
2 Picture the question in your mind.		**Imagine the time of year. What's he saying? Oh yes, April showers ...**
3 Picture the question again.		**Is it certain to rain in April? No, but it's possible. It's not impossible, and I would say there is more than an even chance it will rain in April.**
4 Does the answer look sensible? If so, place your arrow on the scale.		**I'll put my arrow pointing towards 'more likely' as that seems most sensible.**

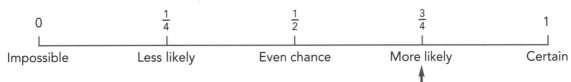

'It will rain at least once during April.'

Now let's try a probability question that asks for a mathematically correct answer.

These coloured balls were placed in a bag:

5 pink   30 blue   2 green   3 brown

Estimate the chance that the first ball to be taken out of the bag will be a blue ball and mark it on the probability scale.

1 Read the question then read it again.

Words and numbers to think about. What is the question asking you to do?

2 Picture the question in your mind.

Try to picture the different coloured balls going into the bag.

3 Add up the total number of balls.

$5 + 30 + 2 + 3 = 40$

4 How many of them are blue?

There are 30 blue balls. So there are 30 blue balls out of 40.

5 Express your probability as a fraction, decimal or percentage. This is important!

This can be expressed as a fraction, percentage or decimal:
$\frac{3}{4}$ 75%   0.75

6 Decide where to place your arrow.

Draw the arrow three quarters of the way along the line. Be accurate here because the probability scale is clearly marked.

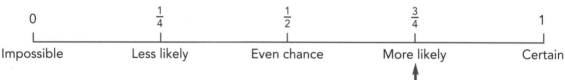

0	$\frac{1}{4}$	$\frac{1}{2}$	$\frac{3}{4}$	1
Impossible	Less likely	Even chance	More likely	Certain

First ball will be blue.

Practice questions

1 On a dice, what is the probability of throwing a 6?

2 James spins this spinner.

What is the probability he gets a 3?

Simple formulae

Formulae can be written in words or in letters. To achieve Level 5 you may be required to make up your own formulae in the tests. This is easier than it sounds! Let's start by working through this example.

Let's practise!

> Here is a formula for finding the total cost of a pay-as-you-go mobile phone call.
>
> T = £0.25 × M   T = total cost
>
> Each minute costs 25p.
>
> M = number of minutes

> Now write a formula for finding the cost of one call when the total cost of N calls is £2.25 and the cost of one call is C.

1	Read the question then read it again.	**Lots to read and think about here!**
2	What am I being asked to do?	**Write a formula for finding the cost of one call using £2.25, and 'N' and 'C'.**
3	It will help if you say the formula to yourself.	**The total cost is £2.25. So … the cost of one call is £2.25, divided by the number of calls, N.**
4	Change your logical statement into a simple formula. Say it to yourself when you write it down.	**The cost of one call … C** **… is the total cost … £2.25** **… divided by (÷) the total number of calls. N** **C = £2.25 ÷ N OR C = £2.25/N**

Tips	★ Talk through your formula in your head. ★ Think clearly. ★ Take it step by step.	★ It helps to use only letters that relate to the information in the question, e.g. C = cost.

A simple formula is often used to find out the total cost of items bought.

Achieved?

☺ 😐 ☹

In words this formula can be written:

'The total cost is the price of one item multiplied by the number of those items bought.'

In letter formulae this could be written as: **T = N × P**

T = total cost   N = number of items bought   P = price of each item

Practice questions

Use the T = N × P formula to work out these questions.

① What is the value of **T** if **N** = 8 and **P** = £1.75?

② What is the value of **N** if **T** = £60 and **P** = £3?

③ What is the value of **P** if **T** = £72 and **N** = 9?

Example question

James and Melissa are playing a number game. James gives Melissa a number which she changes using a rule:

'I take James's number and multiply it by 9 then subtract 8.'

Write a formula to show the process Melissa goes through to get to her answer.

Use J for James's number and M for Melissa's answer.

M = $(J \times 9) - 8$

Practice question

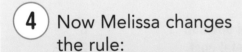

I take James's number and multiply it by 7 then add 7.

④ Now Melissa changes the rule:

Write a formula to show the process Melissa goes through to get to her answer.

Use J for James's number and M for Melissa's answer.

M =

| Tip | ★ If a number and a letter are next to each other, e.g. 4N, it means they are multiplied. Why is the × (multiply) symbol left out? Because it could get confused with the letter x!! |

Solving problems

Introduction

The reason for learning all the different mathematical skills (multiplying, dividing, measuring, estimating, and so on) is so you can use them to solve mathematical problems.

Imagine learning all the shots in tennis, like the serve, the volley, the backhand and forehand, but never actually getting to play a game! Only by using your shots in a match will you learn to be a tennis player. Likewise, only by using your mathematical skills will you learn to be a mathematician!

The flow chart on page 54 is designed to guide you when tackling a maths problem. It will help organise your thinking, but it won't tell you the answer – that's for you to work out for yourself.

The next few pages contain problems for you to solve. Work through the examples first and then have a go at the practice questions using the flow chart approach.

Good luck!

Problem solving

Number

These questions are all about your number skills. You must use them in the right way though!

Measures

These questions are all about real situations: going on a journey, the amount of milk a family drinks in a week, and so on.

Shape and space

These questions all require you to use your knowledge about shapes, both 2-D and 3-D.

Handling data

These questions often ask you to find out information from a table or chart. They will also ask you to explain how you found out the answer!

The problem-solving flow chart

1 Read the question then read it again.

Read the question carefully. Twice. Let the words and numbers 'sink in'.

2 Write the numbers and highlight any key words.

Write down any numbers and key words. It might help to draw a picture or diagram.

3 Can you estimate an answer?

This depends on the question. Try to estimate using the numbers and words you jotted down in step 2.

4 Which calculations do you need to do?

Work out if you need to use +, −, × or ÷ and check if you need to do more than one calculation.

5 Work out the problem.

Do any calculations needed. Make sure you are answering the problem.

6 Is your answer sensible?

Read the question again and check that your answer is realistic. If not, go back to step 2.

Tips	★ Remember your 'checking the answer' skills. ★ Think clearly and write clearly. ★ Present your work so it shows what you have done. ★ Work step by step. ★ Make a problem easier (e.g. Find 24 lots of 6. Try finding 4 lots first then 20 lots).	★ Take a reasonable guess at what you think might happen. ★ Think HOW you are working. Change your method if something isn't working. ★ Look for patterns in your maths.

Solving number problems

Let's practise!

The numbers in row 2 of this triangle of pool balls have been found from the two numbers directly above them using a rule. Fill in the missing numbers and write the rule.

Row 1	84	72	88	44
Row 2		78	80	66
Row 3				
Row 4				

Rule: _____

1 Read the question then read it again.

There are two things to do to complete this question – 'find the missing numbers' and 'write the rule'.

2 Picture the words and numbers. What do they mean?

How are these numbers 'linked'? When we have worked it out, we need to explain how.

3 Highlight key words and phrases.

'numbers in row 2', 'found from the two numbers directly above'.

4 Can you estimate an answer?

No, because the answer is not immediately obvious.

5 What calculations do you need to do?

Work step by step. Start with 84 and 72. What do we have to do to get 78?
84 + 72 = or 84 – 72 =

6 What is the answer to your calculations? Show how you got your answer.

84 + 72 = 156 and 84 – 72 = 12
Look at our answers. Can we see any 'link' with 78? Yes! 156 is double 78 or 78 is half 156. We have found the rule!

7 What is the answer to the original problem? Write it in full.

The rule is add the two numbers together and divide the total by two. We can also fill in the missing numbers.
(78 + 80) ÷ 2 = 79 and (80 + 66) ÷ 2 = 73 so (79 + 73) ÷ 2 = 76

8 Is your answer a sensible one?

Yes, we can test our rule throughout the triangle. It works!

Practice questions

Use the flow chart to help you solve these number problems.

Achieved?
😊 😐 ☹

1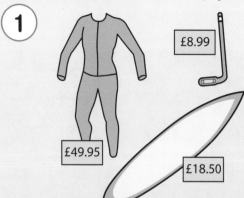

£8.99

£49.95

£18.50

Talib had £100. He chose a surfboard and a wetsuit. He received a 20% discount of the total price. How much money did he have left?

2 There are 3 girls for every 4 boys in Class 6A. If there are 28 children in the class, how many of them are girls?

3 Daniel starts at zero and counts in steps of 9.

0, 9, 18, 27, 36

a) He says the number 563 will be in his sequence.

Is he correct?   YES   NO

Explain how you know.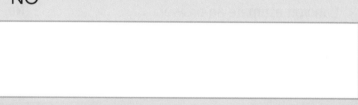

b) What is the first number greater than 700 that would be in his sequence?

4 Put the numbers 1 to 9 into this grid so that the sum of the numbers of the columns, rows and the diagonals each equal 15. Investigate other magic squares.

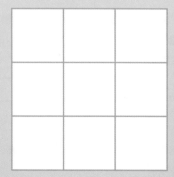

Solving measures problems

Let's try this simple measures problem.

Let's practise!

Here is a list of ingredients for Jimmy's jam tarts. It makes 12 jam tarts.

180 g plain flour   6 teaspoons of water

80 g of butter   120 g of strawberry jam

12 fresh strawberries

Jimmy is having some extra friends round for tea and wants to make 15 of his special tarts. Can you change the amount of each ingredient so he cooks enough tarts?

1	Read the question then read it again.	**Change the amounts of 5 ingredients …**
2	Picture the words and numbers. What do they mean?	**We could draw each item.**
3	Highlight key words and phrases.	**Change the amounts so there are enough tarts for 15 instead of 12 … That's an increase of 25%!**
4	Can you estimate an answer?	**Not easy as there are lots of ingredients, but we know we are adding a 'quarter as much again' to each ingredient.**
5	What calculations do you need to do?	**25% of each – 180 g, 80 g, 6 teaspoons, 120 g, 12 strawberries.**
6	What is the answer to your calculations? Show how you got your answer.	**25% of 180 g = 45 g** **25% of 80 g = 20 g** **25% of 6 teaspoons = 1.5 teaspoons** **25% of 120 g = 30 g** **25% of 12 strawberries = 3 strawberries** **Add these to the amounts for 12.**
7	What is the answer to the original problem? Write it in full.	**Jimmy would need 225 g of plain flour, 100 g of butter, 7.5 teaspoons of water, 150 g of jam and 15 strawberries.**
8	Is your answer a sensible one?	**Yes, we have increased the ingredients by the correct amounts.**

Practice questions

1

A tub contains 12 identical cups and weighs 900 g.

The empty tub weighs 36 g.

What is the weight of each cup?

2

perimeter = 498 mm

(not to scale)

A square has a perimeter of 498 mm.

What is the length of each side in cm?

3

Hannah has a jigsaw puzzle that is 83 cm long and 30 cm wide. If each puzzle piece is 3 mm thick, what is the volume of the jigsaw puzzle?

4 During a holiday, the Chang family put 28 litres of petrol of petrol into the car 6 times. When they left on holiday, the car held 24 litres of petrol. When they returned home it held 13 litres of petrol. How much petrol did they use altogether on holiday?

Solving shape and space problems

Let's try a tricky shape and space problem.

Let's practise!

How many equilateral triangles can you see in this diagram?

Show your method:

1	Read the question then read it again.	Study the words and the shape. Think past the obvious.
2	Picture the words and numbers. What do they mean?	It would help to sketch the shape on paper. You will need to work in a logical, methodical way. Think step by step!
3	Highlight key words and phrases.	How many. We are going to need the exact number of triangles to be correct. Miss one and we're wrong!
4	Can you estimate an answer?	We can see 17 in front of us (16 little ones and the big one). 5 hidden, 22 in total.
5	What calculations do you need to do?	Work in a logical way using a table. How many 1 triangles are there? How many 4 triangles are there? And so on …
6	What is the answer to your calculations? Show how you got your answer.	(see table below)

Number of smaller triangles in the big triangle	1	4	9	16	Total
Quantity seen	16	7	3	1	27

7	What is the answer to the original problem? Write it in full.	We can see 27 equilateral triangles in the diagram.
8	Is your answer a sensible one?	It looks sensible because we worked in a step-by-step way. Our estimate was quite close and a logical approach has given us the correct answer.

Practice questions

1 Rachel uses square slabs to make a path with this pattern.

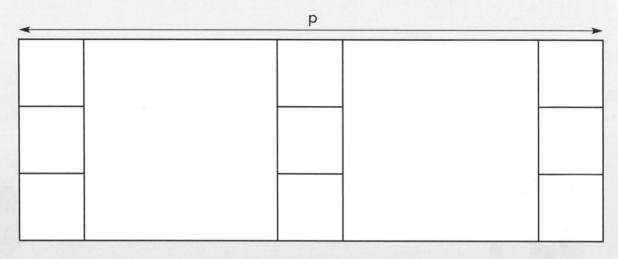

If the large square has a side length of 84 cm, what is length p?

2 This tile is turned 90° clockwise.

Complete the tile in its new position.

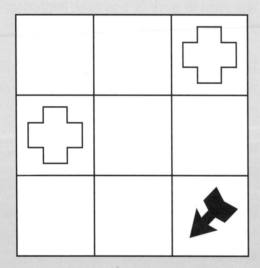
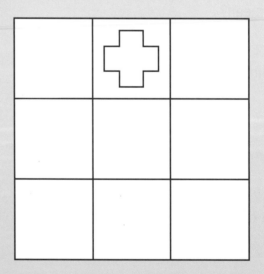

3 A quadrilateral has one pair of parallel sides and one pair of equal sides.

Name the shape.

Key facts

Counting and understanding number

Place value
- Each number is made up of digits. The position of the digit in a number gives its value.

Hundreds	Tens	Units	tenths	hundredths
7	8	4	3	5

$= 700 + 80 + 4 + \frac{3}{10} + \frac{5}{100} = 784.35$

Rounding
- When rounding, remember that 5 goes up! $6.785 = 6.79$

Negative numbers
- Integers are just whole numbers.
- When counting from negative up to positive or from positive down to negative, **remember to count 0!**
- When counting on a number line, count to the right when adding and to the left when subtracting.

Fractions
- A fraction is part of a whole number.

$\frac{1}{2}$ the numerator / the denominator

The numerator tells you how many equal parts are used.
The denominator tells you how many equal parts there are.

Reducing a fraction to its simplest form
- To reduce a fraction to its simplest form, find a common factor which you can divide into the numerator and the denominator. For example,

$$\frac{3 \div 3}{9 \div 3} = \frac{1}{3}$$

Fraction, decimal and percentage equivalents
- Remember as many of these as you can.

Fraction	$\frac{1}{2}$	$\frac{1}{10}$	$\frac{1}{4}$	$\frac{3}{4}$	Nearly $\frac{1}{3}$
Decimal	0.5	0.1	0.25	0.75	0.33
Percentage	50%	10%	25%	75%	33%

The vocabulary of ratio and proportion
- Ratio is 'to every'.
- Proportion is 'in every'.
- Reduce ratios and proportions to their lowest form.

Knowing and using number facts
- **Tables:** it is essential that you know these really well.
- **Squares:** numbers made when a number is multiplied by itself.
- **Multiples:** numbers that have been multiplied by a given number.
- **Factors:** numbers that can divide into a given number without leaving a remainder.

Checking your answers
- Inverse means opposite!
- Check addition by subtraction – and vice versa.
- Check division by multiplication – and vice versa.
- Use 'friendly numbers' when estimating: 2, 5, 10, etc.

Calculating
- Multiplying numbers by 10 and 100: Push the digits to the left once for × 10 and twice for ÷ 100.
- Dividing numbers by 10 and 100: Push the digits to the right once for ÷ 10 and twice for ÷ 100.
- Addition and subtraction of decimals:
  1. Line up the decimal points when you write out the sum.
  2. Fill empty places with a 0.
  3. Remember to put the decimal point in your answer!
- Multiplication and division of decimals:
  1. × and ÷ are opposites
  2. Remember – there must be the same number of digits after the decimal point in the answer as there are in the question.

Brackets
- Always do the brackets in equations first.

Choosing your method
- Remember to look at the numbers you are working with. You might be able to use a good mental strategy rather than a written method, or it might be best to use a calculator.

Understanding shape

3-D shapes
- Vertices are corners.
- Faces are flat surfaces.
- Edges are edges!

2-D shapes
- Polygons have all straight sides.
- Regular polygons have sides all the same length.
- Parallel lines never meet – think of a train track!
- Perpendicular lines make a right angle.

Triangles
- An isosceles triangle has TWO EQUAL SIDES AND TWO EQUAL ANGLES. Picture an isosceles triangle as an arrow! A scalene triangle has THREE SIDES OF DIFFERENT LENGTHS and THREE ANGLES OF DIFFERENT SIZES. When picturing a scalene triangle, think of scaling a mountain that has an easy way up or a more difficult side to climb!

Moving 2-D shapes
- When drawing reflections, remember to keep the correct distance from the mirror line.
- Remember, rotational symmetry is just working out how many ways the shape can fit EXACTLY on top of itself.
- When translating a shape move it across, then up or down.

Angles
- Acute angle is between 0 and 89°
- Right angle = 90°
- Obtuse angle is between 91 and 179°
- Straight line = 180°
- Reflex angle is between 181 and 359°

Coordinates
- Always read ALONG the x axis and then UP the y axis.
- Always write (x) before (y), i.e. (x, y)

Measuring

Metric and imperial conversions
- 1 litre = 1.8 pints
- 1 kilogram = 2.2 lbs (pounds)
- 1 pound = 0.454 kg
- 1 mile = 1.6 km
- 5 miles = 8 km
- 1 foot = 30 cm
- 1 metre = 3 feet 3 inches
- 1 inch = 2.5 cm

Measures
- Milli = $\frac{1}{1000}$

- Centi = $\frac{1}{100}$
- Deci = $\frac{1}{10}$
- Dec = 10
- Cent = 100
- Kilo = 1000

Perimeter
- Perimeter is the distance all the way round the edge of a shape.

Area
- Area is the space covered up by the shape.
- Count the squares and remember area is always measured in units squared (cm^2, mm^2, m^2)

Area of a rectangle
- Area of a rectangle = length (L) × width (W)

Reading scales
CAREFULLY work out what each mark on the scale is worth.

Handling data

Pictograms
- With pictograms **picture = number**

e.g. ▽ = 20 ice creams ⌒ = 10 ice creams

Mean, median, range, mode
- Mean = sum of all values divided by number of values
- Median = middle number in sequence (always write down in order first)
- Range = difference between highest and lowest number
- Mode = most common value

Charts and graphs
- Be careful and accurate. Use a sharp pencil.
- Pie charts are good for percentages, fractions or decimals.

Probability scale
- Always goes from 0 to 1 (you need fractions/decimals here).

Using and applying mathematics

Simple formulae
- Talk through the formula in your head. It will make it easier.

Number patterns
- Check the difference between the numbers to find the pattern.

Answers

Page 9 – Predicting sequences
1) 59, 71   2) 7, 17   3) 1, –3   4) 11, 17

Page 10 – Calculators
1) 12,075   2) 4086.732   3) 862.25   4) 546.54   5) 1257.5   6) 10,300

Page 12 – The 24-hour clock
1) 4 hours 45 mins   2) 7 hours 27 minutes   3) 03:07

Page 13 – Reading scales
A = 0.8 km or 800 m   B = 1.3 km or 1300 km   C = 2.6 km or 2600 m

Page 16 – Negative numbers
1) a) –5°C   b) –8°C   c) –10°C
2) –20, –18, –16, –7, 6, 16
3) –4 and 2 circled
4)

Temperature in Moscow (°C)	2	–5	–12	0
Temperature in Oslo (°C)	10	3	–4	8

Page 17 – Reducing fractions
1) $\frac{2}{3}$ 2) $\frac{3}{5}$ 3) $\frac{8}{13}$ 4) $\frac{5}{6}$ 5) $\frac{4}{7}$

Page 20 – Writing one number as a percentage of another
1) a) 65%   b) 52%   c) 22.5%
2) 70%   3) 84%

Page 21 – Checking your answers
1) 828   2) 2695   3) 7239   4) 524

Page 22 – Checking your answers – rounding up or down
1) 12,625   2) 3008   3) 7926   4) 18

Page 23 – Decimal numbers and tables
1) 4.2   2) 0.0064   3) 0.24   4) 0.054   5) 0.036   6) 0.35

Page 24 – Number properties
2, 3, 5, 7, 11, 13, 17, 19, 23, 29, 31, 37, 41, 43, 47, 53, 59, 61, 67, 71, 73, 79, 83, 89, 97

Page 26 – Using brackets
1) 5.76   2) 10,176   3) 8   4) 330   5) 27   6) 3

Page 27 – Adding and subtracting decimals
1) 37.85   2) 307.68   3) 101.38   4) 76.293

Page 28 – Multiplying and dividing decimals
1) 60.696   2) 146.5   3) 237.16   4) 3019.53   5) 9.4   6) 93.06

Page 29 – Long multiplication
1) 19,875   2) 23,870   3) 14,652

Page 30 – Long division
1) 45   2) 36   3) 29

Page 31 – Fractions of amounts
1) 75   2) 52   3) 115   4) 352   5) 72
6) 112   7) 150   8) 252   9) 240   10) 258

Page 40 – Angles at a point
1) 61°   2) 150°   3) 74°   4) 15°

Page 41 – Units of measure
1) 5 litres (accept 4.5 litres)   2) 9–10 kilograms

Page 42 – Units of measure
1) 50,000 ml   2) 7843 cm   3) 46.752 kg

Page 44 – The area of a rectangle
1) 2050 cm²   2) 106 m²

Page 45 – Finding the mean and median
1) a) 7   b) 55   c) 412   d) 306
2) a) 6   b) 5   c) 57

Page 47 – Conversion graphs
a) ★ 88   b) ★ 64

Page 48 – Pie charts
a) $\frac{1}{4}$ b) $\frac{5}{8}$ c) $\frac{1}{2}$

Page 50 – Probability
1) $\frac{1}{6}$ 2) $\frac{3}{8}$

Page 52 – Simple formulae
1) T = £14   2) N = 20   3) P = £8   4) Formula M = (J x 7) + 7

Page 56 – Solving number problems
1) £45.24   2) 12
3) a) No, 563 is not divisible by 9 because its digits add up to 14 (which is not divisible by 9)
   b) 702
4)

8	1	6
3	5	7
4	9	2

Page 58 – Solving measures problems
1) 72 g   2) 12.45 cm   3) 747 cm³   4) 179 litres

Page 60 – Solving shape and space problems
1) 252 cm   2)   3) trapezium

After twenty-three years as a school, the House, together with ninety acres of parkland, was purchased by Newport Borough Council, and in 1976 a major programme of restoration and refurnishing began.

This was a demanding but challenging task. The House was almost devoid of its original contents. There was very little furniture, few pictures, only one carpet and no curtains! The interior had also suffered from the wear and tear of a generation of schoolchildren: the panelling had usefully doubled as notice boards and the chalk imprint of blackboard dusters splattered the overmantel paintings. Moreover, the

structure of t
with dry rot a

However, over the past twenty-two years, tremendous progress has been made, and with the continuing financial support of CADW (Welsh Historic Monuments), the Wales Tourist Board, the Countryside Commission, the Council of Museums in Wales, the Friends of Tredegar House, and many private individuals and institutions, Newport County Borough Council should be able to fulfil its aim of restoring not only the House but also the Home Farm, Stables, Gardens and Park to something like their original appearance.

An early portrait of an unknown Morgan child

1

THE HOUSE

The visitor approached the medieval house from the north-west, passing through 'The Great Gate' into 'The Great Bowling Green', then through a second gate into 'The Middle Court', and finally through into 'The Inner Court' via the gate in the screen wall. The house was arranged around the three remaining sides of 'The Inner Court', its windows looking inwards into the courtyard itself.

Tredegar House is the finest Restoration house in Wales. The principal façade consists of two storeys with cellars below and attics above and with the entrance centrally placed and flanked by two projecting pavilions. The use of brick is worth noting, for brick was a building material rarely used in Wales at this time, owing to the ready availability of stone. The oldest part of the House (now the Servants' Hall) dates from the late fifteenth or early sixteenth centuries and originally formed part of a substantial medieval manor house.

A copy of an early seventeenth century plan of the medieval house, shows the arrangement of the Tudor gardens. This copy was made by Octavius Morgan (1802-1888), brother of the first Lord Tredegar and a noted antiquary, and is the only source of information relating to the medieval house

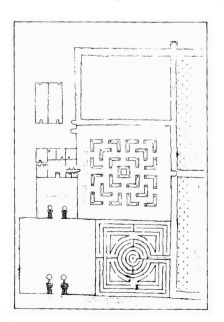

The main seventeenth century doorway (pictured above) is something of a rarity. The broken pediment is surmounted by a lion and a griffin, the supporters of the Morgan coat of arms which are incorporated on the carved shield centred between, and supported by a pair of spiral columns entwined with laurel leaves in the style of the Italian Baroque. It is particularly unusual to find such columns on a seventeenth century building designed for domestic use, for they are more often associated with ecclesiastical structures

Between c.1664 and 1672 Tredegar was remodelled on an unusually grand scale. The north-east wing of the medieval house was completely rebuilt and the screen wall replaced by an additional wing which was designed as the principal façade. The house thus continued to face north-west but, instead of looking inwards into the inner courtyard, its windows looked out over the gardens and park beyond.

It seems probable that Tredegar was designed and built by an unknown designer-craftsman; a mason, bricklayer or carpenter who was familiar enough with current building styles to design, as well as supervise, the building of the house.

The ground floor windows are treated in a similar manner to the doorway, with broken pediments surmounted by a lion and a griffin flanking an heraldic cartouche, a style of decoration which may have been influenced by the work of Inigo Jones at Wilton House, Wiltshire

The first floor windows are embellished beneath with swags of fruit, a decorative motif for which the closest known parallels can be found only in Holland on such buildings as the Mauritshuis in the Hague and the Town Hall, Amsterdam

3

SIDE HALL

Title detail (left): The set of late eighteenth century mahogany hall chairs are original to the House and display the family crest, a stag's head

The seated figure of Sir Charles Morgan (1760-1846) is by J. E. Thomas and was the model for the life-size bronze statue erected in Newport in 1850

The Delft chimney tiles in the Side Hall are probably nineteenth century and illustrate the traditional skills of horsemanship

This room was described in the 1688 inventory as '*the Drawing Room that is hang'd with Gilt Leather*'. The framed piece of gilt leather mounted above the entrance to the Dining Room may well be part of these original wall hangings. They may have been removed in the 1860s by Octavius Morgan, brother of the first Lord Tredegar, when the room was remodelled as an entrance hall: a doorway replaced the window, a porch was added and the ceiling lowered. The New Hall, the seventeenth century entrance hall, became a drawing room.

The room was redecorated in 1979, using a hand-blocked wallpaper of a design circa 1870, and is being furnished as a Victorian entrance hall.

This room is mentioned in only one of the surviving inventories, that for 1698, in which it is listed as '*The Drinking Roome*'. It was then appropriately furnished with ten old leather chairs and an oval table.

In more recent times, it was the office of Lord Tredegar's personal secretary, but is now furnished as an early nineteenth century Morning Room for the use of the ladies of the House.

Most of the furniture is of rosewood, including the secretaire-cabinet (*c.*1820) and the centre table and side table (both *c.*1830) just inside the door. Rosewood was a wood much favoured by furniture makers in the early decades of the nineteenth century for it has a very pronounced and attractive grain. The pair of Pontypool japanware candlesticks (lacquered metalware produced in Pontypool *c.*1750-1850) display the Morgan family crest and are on loan from the National Museum of Wales.

MORNING ROOM

Title detail (left) - a section of the room's carpet

Below - a portrait of Lady Rachel Cavendish Morgan (1697-1780)

The fitted '*Brussels*' carpet was copied from a carpet made in Paris in 1829. It has been woven in the traditional manner in twenty-seven inch strips which have been pattern matched, sewn together and bordered with a narrower strip of a complementary design. It is known as a '*Brussels*' carpet owing to the fact that the pile is left looped, rather than cut, for a '*Brussels*' weave was thought to be more hardwearing.

5

In the late seventeenth century this room was known as *'The New Parlour'* to distinguish it from the old parlour which survived in the medieval part of the building. Although it was used by the family for dining it was not until about the middle of the eighteenth century that it replaced the Brown Room as the main dining room for the House. The room is now being presented as a dining room of the Victorian period, but in the *'antiquarian style'*. Some items of furniture are nineteenth century copies of seventeenth century pieces. Others are earlier pieces which have been subsequently altered. The room is panelled from floor to ceiling and has a calm, classical appearance.

DINING ROOM

Title detail: 'The Tredegar Salt'

The simple vine and grape motif dividing the lower panels, the delicate acanthus panel incorporating a lion and a griffin (supporters of the Morgan coat of arms) beneath the mantelshelf, and the festoons of fruit at cornice level on the same wall are the only details of exuberance. The serving hatch linking the Dining Room and Great Kitchen via the Bells Passage and Kitchen Corridor, is disguised in the panelling to the left of the doorway.

The ceiling, though nineteenth century, is sympathetic to the room and a good example of the period. The centre circle consists of a great wreath of trailing vine leaves, grapes, pomegranates, artichokes and flowers, which provide cover for a fox, a lion, a griffin and many playful cherubs, one of which carries a flag bearing the Morgan crest.

The chandelier, like the electric light fittings in most of the other rooms, was installed c.1921 when electricity was introduced to the House.

In the middle window of the north-east wall are two panels of late seventeenth century stained glass, depicting on the left, the arms of the Stuart kings, and on the right, the arms of the Morgan family, incorporating 24 quarterings.

On the dining table (c.1840) is a part Copeland dinner service. It was ordered by the family on 6 August 1853 and displays the family colours, blue and gold and their motto, *Deus Nobiscum Quis Contra Nos* (God is with us, who can be against us?).

The New Hall circa 1830,
showing Sir Charles Morgan and his family

New Hall

This was the main entrance hall for Tredegar from the late seventeenth century until the remodelling of the Side Hall in the nineteenth century. It is described in the 1688 inventory as '*The New Hall*' to distinguish it from the hall in the medieval building. The Hall served a variety of purposes, acting as a reception room for distinguished visitors and large companies, as an ante-chamber in which visitors of lower rank could wait and amuse themselves, and as an additional dining room.

The New Hall in 1908,
showing the original ceiling

In the late seventeenth century this was the State Dining Room, a very formal room used only on special occasions. The family generally dined either in the New Parlour or in their bedchambers or adjacent closets. The room was clearly designed to impress for the carved oak decoration is amazingly lavish. The carving was probably executed in the 1680s. The style of carving has much in common with seventeenth century Flemish and French renaissance work and is possibly derived from a continental engraver's pattern book, though the execution of the work is idiosyncratically English and '*mannerist*' in design. Each panel is separated vertically by a '*pilaster*', intricately carved with scrolling acanthus and clambering putti (naked infants) who appear to be hanging on for their lives. The upper and lower panels are each separated at waist height by a wide band of foliage, interwoven with a curious mixture of serpents, lions, winged cherubs, '*gargoyles*', and heraldic shields. The band of foliage is broken between the vertical panels by a series of exquisitely carved heads, half human, half animal. The upper panels are surmounted by scrolling split pediments containing stylised busts of Roman emperors.

Title detail (below): One of the room's elaborate oak carvings; this one is reputed to be a caricature of King Charles I as a mouse

Brown Room

The doorways are treated in a similar but more elaborate manner, the painted plaster busts of the Emperor Augustus and his wife, Livia, being supported by intricately carved trophies of arms and musical instruments, respectively.

Far right: an early portrait of an unknown Morgan woman

This was the most important room in the House for eating during the seventeenth century. Here spectacular feasts would be served to important guests. The dishes were placed on the table in a formal geometric pattern and blocks of wood were often put under the cloth so that dishes could be displayed at different levels. Food was eaten off silver, pewter or pottery plates. Glass began to replace metal, clay and wooden drinking cups and was used to serve wine, sweetmeats, jellies and syllabubs.

The ceiling is a nineteenth century replacement. The original late seventeenth century ceiling collapsed in 1848. This was decorated in a similar manner to the ceiling in the Gilt Room, with an oval frame containing an allegorical painting illustrating 'The Tribute of the Gods to Flora and Zephyr'

Described in the 1688 inventory as '*the Gilted Roome*', it probably served as a reception room to which the assembled company retired after dinner on formal occasions. The decoration is so rich as to make it stand apart in one's memory from the remaining rooms in the house.

The pine panelling is grained to imitate walnut and most of the upper panels are painted. The mouldings and carvings which separate the panels are all gilded, the swags of fruit (like those above the chimney-piece in the Dining Room) reflecting the exterior stone dressings beneath the first floor windows.

The chimney-piece likewise glitters with gilding and has the general character of an Italian Baroque altarpiece. Grotesque, half-human figures clambering among the mass of vegetation surrounding the chimney-piece seem to look over the room with an expression of complete amazement. Hidden amongst the twisting foliage beneath the centre of the mantelshelf are carved the initials of William Morgan, who was probably responsible for rebuilding the house. The twisted columns with their gilded Corinthian capitals are pine, marbled to imitate stone.

The elaborate stucco and painted ceiling is the only surviving seventeenth century ceiling on the ground floor. The painting is probably copied from an engraving published by Tetius in 1647 of part of the ceiling in the Gran-Salone of the Palazzo Barberrini in Rome, entitled *The Glorification of Pope Urban VIII's Reign* by Pietro da Cortona. The painting illustrates how Pope Urban, through his piety and wisdom, overcame lust and intemperance. Lust is represented by a naked female figure surrounded by winged cupids, Intemperance by Silenus, father of Bacchus, god of wine, all watched over by Wisdom. The painting is contained within an enormous oval composed of various fruits and flowers, the whole surrounded by a rectangle of scrolling acanthus leaves, while at each end is a somewhat grotesque figure with long, flowing beard and hair.

GILT GROOM

GREAT STAIRCASE

The portrait at the top of the stairs is of Sir Charles Gould Morgan (1726-1806)

A detail from the painting on the stairs of Sir Charles Kemeys of Cefn Mabli, and William Morgan of Machen and Tredegar

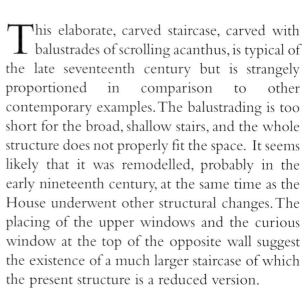

This elaborate, carved staircase, carved with balustrades of scrolling acanthus, is typical of the late seventeenth century but is strangely proportioned in comparison to other contemporary examples. The balustrading is too short for the broad, shallow stairs, and the whole structure does not properly fit the space. It seems likely that it was remodelled, probably in the early nineteenth century, at the same time as the House underwent other structural changes. The placing of the upper windows and the curious window at the top of the opposite wall suggest the existence of a much larger staircase of which the present structure is a reduced version.

Located at the western corner of the state wing, directly above the Gilt Room, this room was designed as the best bedchamber and was intended only for the use of distinguished guests. The room has recently been restored and redecorated and is being refurnished as the best of the late seventeenth century bedchambers. The panelling has been painted a very dark greyish green, an authentic seventeenth century colour appropriately known as '*drab*'.

The plaster ceiling is one of the few seventeenth century ceilings to survive in the house and is perhaps the most attractive. It consists of a central oval of fruit and leaves contained within a plain rectangle and surrounded by a series of smaller panels, again decorated with fruit and leaf motifs.

Title detail (below): Eighteenth century Dutch tiles illustrating the skills of horsemanship

BEST CHAMBER

PASSING ROOM

The Passing Room has retained its original name through to the present century and was so called because it had to be passed through in order to reach the Best Chamber beyond. However, this arrangement was later found to be too inconvenient, and consequently, some time in the late eighteenth century, a corridor was inserted, the room narrowed and the original ceiling removed. Like the Best Chamber, the Passing Room was most probably intended for the use of guests. It is now furnished as an early eighteenth century interior.

The tapestry, on loan from Swansea City Council, is English and dates from about 1710 and the very impressive chest on chest, on loan from the Victoria & Albert Museum, is a little later in date, about 1740, and was possibly made in Ireland

Title detail (right): Photograph of Evan Viscount Tredegar

K ING'S ROOM

This room was probably named after King Gould, Sir Charles Gould Morgan's father, who was no doubt a frequent visitor to Tredegar House in the late eighteenth century.

The room has been refurnished as an example of a twentieth century comfortable 'country house' interior to provide a backdrop for the display of later material relating to Tredegar and Evan Morgan in particular. Towards the end of the 1930s the room was used by Evan Viscount Tredegar. As a young man he had been converted to the Roman Catholic faith and eventually became a chamberlain to the Pope, a lay appointment necessitating his presence in Rome for one month every year. Yet, in spite of his religious faith, he still felt able to dabble in black magic, assisted by an old friend, Aleister Crowley, the occultist, who was a frequent visitor to Tredegar. Many a strange thing is said to have happened here!

RED ROOM

Described in the 1698 inventory as 'the young Master's Chamber', it was more recently the bedroom of Princess Olga Dolgorouky, second wife of Evan Viscount Tredegar. The distinctive *Biedermeier* mahogany wash-stand was made in Germany, c. 1840 and is matched by a handsome wardrobe of the same period.

The red silk damask wall hangings and curtains, after which the room is named, are new, but are exact copies of the original nineteenth century damask which had faded and suffered at the hands of a generation of schoolchildren

BLUE ROOM

Used by Princess Olga as her private sitting room, the Blue Room, like the Red Room and King's Room, has been refurnished as an example of a twentieth century *country house* interior. The silk damask, though again a modern copy, has been hand-woven and not machined. The settee is original to the house but has recently been re-upholstered. In the late 17th century the room was variously called 'The Press Chamber' and 'The Working Roome' and contained *presses* or cupboards for storing linen, hangings, clothes, etc.

Godfrey Morgan survived the Charge of the Light Brigade (from a painting in the Side Hall), in 1854. The saddle cloth of his horse 'Sir Briggs' rests here alongside a bronze of Godfrey as a soldier and a portrait above, shows him with his favourite Skye terrier 'Peeps'

MASTER'S DRESSING ROOM

The gilded and painted leather screen is from Hill Court, near Ross-on-Wye

The curtains are of the same material as those in the Gilt Room, a wool worsted 'camlet', but trimmed with a bell fringe

Trimmings, such as braids, fringes and tassels, were lavishly applied to curtains, hangings and upholstery in the late seventeenth century, and, because they were so expensive, reflected the client's wealth

A dressing room since the seventeenth century, the room contained in 1692:

'One skreene of Guilt Leather, one large Looking glass, two great Caine Chaires, two small Caine Chaires, one Table of Drawers and one Chest of Drawers.'

The furnishing scheme for the room is modelled on this inventory.

The Master's Bedchamber has been refurnished as an early eighteenth century bedchamber

MASTER'S BEDCHAMBER

John Morgan - one of the family portraits that hang in the room

The bed, on loan from the Victoria and Albert Museum, dates from about 1720, though only the tester (top) is original. The curtain hangings, bedcover and valance are recent replacements, but the fabric and braids have been carefully copied. The material, again a wool worsted fabric, has been crushed so that the ribbed weave reflects the light unevenly to produce a wavy effect known as '*watering*'. This '*watered*' or '*moire*' effect can still be seen on the original fabric covering the tester. The walnut veneered chest of drawers (*c.* 1730) to the right of the bed is original to the house and has the Morgan crest and name of Sir Charles Morgan carved into the drawer front.

CEDAR CLOSET

The Cedar Closet is the most precious room on the first floor and the only closet to survive in the house. Closets were small, elegant, lavishly decorated rooms, warm and comfortable, where favoured guests would sometimes be received.

Title detail (above): A specimen of a deadly puffer fish is part of a collection of curios and strange sea creatures displayed in the room

This was almost certainly the Master's Closet and is completely panelled in cedar, a rare and expensive wood, much appreciated for its smell. The panelling conceals a series of cupboards, framed by spiral twist pilasters, topped with intricately carved Corinthian capitals and lion masks. The cupboards may have housed precious valuables such as books, china, curios or documents, an idea which seems to be confirmed by the double barring of the window, the only window in Tredegar to be treated in such a manner.

The painted ceiling, though much restored, dates from the late seventeenth century, and depicts a group of cherubs carrying garlands of fruit and flowers, set against the sky and framed by a border of foliage, amongst which are hidden a monkey, a squirrel, a pair of doves and an exotic bird.

Set into the window is a painted sundial, dated 1672, which could possibly indicate the date by which the re-building of the house was completed, though it could quite easily have been transferred from elsewhere and installed at a later date

BATHROOM

Probably the Master's Study in the late seventeenth century, this room was remodelled as a bathroom c. 1905 and is a delightfully evocative period interior. It was always known as the 'Cow Bathroom' owing to the collection of Staffordshire cows that stood on the marble shelves behind the shower and bath. The fittings were quite advanced for their time and included a bidet and a shower that sprayed out from the sides, as well as from the top. The room has been redecorated following an authentic Edwardian colour scheme.

BELOW STAIRS

"There are 22 servants in the house, of course that does not include those who come in to work everyday. There is a man in the Kitchen who cooks all the meat (the butcher he is called). He prepares all the meat. Then there is a man in the scullery, also a woman kept for washing up, and two stillroom maids, and a woman comes every day to bake the bread. So there are five in the Kitchen and two regularly in the scullery. I am afraid Miss Brown that sounds very much like a fairy tale, but, when I tell you there are fourteen cold meats sent up every day for my Lord's Luncheon including four or five hot dishes, you will understand there is some work to be done in the Kitchen alone! Then my Lord has a clean table cloth for every meal. Is it not ridiculous? Sometimes when he is alone we have twenty three table cloths in the wash in a week and when he has a lot of company we have anywhere from thirty-six to forty. His sister is Lady Hereford of Ludlow, and when she and her daughter come here there is plenty of work for everyone. The sideboard cloths are changed three or four times a week and My Lord has a clean cloth, on every tray taken up to him. I often say if cleanliness would keep any one alive, then Viscount Tredegar would never die."

In a country house as grand as Tredegar, there were just as many rooms *below stairs* as there were *above*, for a whole army of servants was required to run such a house. This fact is made wonderfully clear in the following extract from a letter written in 1891 by a servant at Tredegar to the Housekeeper at Erddig, a country house in North Wales, now owned by the National Trust:

THE BELL'S PASSAGE

The Bell's Passage links the servants' quarters with the family apartments. Along here, food from the Great Kitchen was carried to the serving hatch, located at the end of the passage and then passed into the Dining Room. High on the wall above can be seen the mechanical bell system, installed in the mid-nineteenth century. The pendulum of each bell would still be swinging long after the bell had sounded, so as to ensure that tardy servants knew exactly which bell had been rung. The electrical bell system located beneath was installed in about 1921 but has recently been meticulously restored. Like the mechanical system, it incorporated a separate panel for summoning individual servants such as the Butler and the Housekeeper.

BUTLER'S PANTRY

PLATE SCULLERY

In the late seventeenth century the Butler's Pantry was located adjacent to the Great Staircase but was removed to its present position in the 1820s. It was here more conveniently situated for direct access to both the New Hall and Side Hall entrances and also for the Dining Room and Cellars.

The Butler was not only responsible for answering the front door, receiving and announcing guests and ensuring that they were all well looked after, he was also responsible for supervising the service of food and drink and for ensuring that all the writing tables in the house were well-stocked with pens, inks and stationery.

His pantry was lined with an array of cupboards, in which would have been stored cutlery, drinking glasses and table linen, especially damask napkins and lace-edged tray cloths. These would have been pressed in the mahogany linen press (c.1840) by the under-butler or the groom of the chambers, or by a footman. In the oak clothes cupboard (c.1750) they would have hung their livery (uniforms).

The Plate Scullery leads directly off the Butler's Pantry and gave access to the Plate Safe in which all the silver and gold plate were securely kept. In front of this a bed would have been folded down each night from the tall cupboard on the right for the use of a footman, who would have slept here, guarding the Plate Safe. In the Scullery itself the footmen would have cleaned the family plate, refreshed by a supply of bread and cheese and a mug of ale which was left in the cupboard on the left.

The Great Kitchen was the largest, loftiest, and most important room *'below stairs'*. It needed to be large and lofty in order to ensure that the room was kept reasonably ventilated and cool. Even so, the heat generated by the large roasting range, by the two *'closed'* ranges, and by the charcoal stewing range, each of which was usually lit every morning, must have been quite overpowering by the end of the day.

GREAT KITCHEN

The great roasting range, complete with its elaborate spit mechanism supplied by Messrs. Kent and Tuck of Bath, probably dates from the early nineteenth century. The spits were driven by a *'smoke jack'*, a large iron fan fixed horizontally inside the chimney, made to revolve by the upward rush of hot air from the immense heat of the fire below. The fan was connected by a system of gears to the power shaft, which in turn rotated the spits from which joints of meat or game would be hung for roasting. To the left of the roasting range is a copper boiler, probably dating from the late nineteenth century. The boiler was independently fired and was evidently designed to produce piping hot water which was pumped out under steam pressure. Its purpose is not exactly clear but it seems likely that it fed an exceptionally large steamer via four pipes, the ends of which can still be seen cut off amidst the tiles beneath the zinc canopy. The steamer was most probably used for cooking a variety of puddings, both savoury and sweet, the steam being drawn up through the canopy, together with any accompanying food smells.

In the middle of the wall facing the entrance to the Great Kitchen is an early nineteenth century stewing range, a rare survival. It was roughly equivalent to a modern day '*slow*' cooker but it also served as a warming plate. The range was fired by charcoal, a low burning fuel which was placed on the grids beneath the three removable hot plates. The ashes would fall through into the three arched openings beneath, from which they would eventually be raked out. The charcoal was stored in the two '*cellars*' below. The shelves around the kitchen would have been crowded with copper pans, moulds and utensils, making a wonderful display. Most of the copper seen here in the kitchen is original to Tredegar and many of the pieces are stamped with the letter '*T*'.

In the Scullery, maids and the kitchen '*boy*' would carry out the dirty tasks of washing and preparing fruit and vegetables, gutting fish, plucking and drawing game, and washing and cleaning the various pots, utensils, plates and dishes used for the preparation, cooking and serving of food.

The original fittings were removed, unfortunately, after the house had become a school, but four new lead-lined sinks, complete with draining boards together with sets of shelves and duck boards and a spectacular plate rack have been specially made through the generosity and skills of Noel T. James Limited.

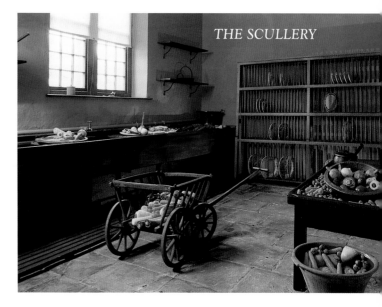

THE SCULLERY

THE PASTRY ROOM

The Pastry Room was located well away from the intense heat of the Great Kitchen. Its cool, slate shelves, work surfaces and flagstone floor provided ideal conditions for the making of pastry for pies and puddings, and for the storage of butter, pies and salted meats. Beneath the internal window is a cold box which, every morning, would have been filled with ice. The ice was delivered to the house in an ice-cart sent from the Ice House in Newport (there is no evidence of an ice house at Tredegar). Before the days of modern refrigeration such a box was essential for the short-term storage of meat or fish already prepared for cooking.

SERVANTS' HALL

Some time in the late eighteenth or early nineteenth century the ground floor of the medieval wing was converted into a Servants' Hall. This room was essentially for the use of the lower servants: the housemaids, the scullery maids, still room maids, footmen, valets, etc. Here at the three large oak refectory tables (c.1750), which are original to Tredegar, they ate all their meals and whiled away what little spare time they were allowed.

The grandest event to take place in the Servants' Hall was the annual Servants' Ball held on Twelfth Night. It was always opened by the head of the family. He would descend the stairs at the end of the hall, which gave access to the main part of the house, and begin the dancing, taking the Housekeeper as his partner. For this occasion the refectory tables would be removed into the courtyard and a mountainous buffet supper would be laid out in the Great Kitchen. The band, a string quartet, would play well into the early hours of the morning and, by the time the party had finished (about 5.30 a.m.), it was time for many of the participants to begin their day's work!

The Still Room came under the control of the Housekeeper and hence was located adjacent to the Housekeeper's Room. Here, under her eagle eye, the Still Room maids would make cordials, jams, jellies, preserves, pickles, and cakes and biscuits for afternoon tea, that most British of institutions, which came into vogue in the 1840s. The Still Room maids would also make up such household necessities as wax polishes and soap flakes.

Through the door on the right is a small sitting room where the Still Room maids could snatch a moment's rest.

HOUSEKEEPER'S ROOM [Spice]

Title detail (left): Part of the Spice Cabinet in the Housekeeper's Room

In the late seventeenth century the Housekeeper's Room was most probably situated in the north-east wing of the house but was relocated here some time in the early nineteenth century to be closer to the Servants' Hall, kitchen wing and tradesmen's entrance.

The Housekeeper was responsible for ensuring that the house was properly cleaned and she liaised with the Master or Mistress regarding their day-to-day requirements. The Housekeeper also looked after the table linen and the china and glassware, and ordered and stored groceries, such as tea, coffee, sugar, preserves and spices. She was consequently responsible for supervising most of the female staff, notably the housemaids, still room maids and laundry maids. It was also a reasonably comfortable room for it was used not only by the Housekeeper but also by the upper servants as a communal sitting room to which they would retire during or after dinner. The main course was usually consumed in the Servants' Hall, but the pudding course was quite often taken in the Housekeeper's Room, the upper servants ceremoniously processing out of the Servants' Hall in strict order of precedence, pudding in hand.

The Middle and Stable Courts appear to overlay the earlier courts of the medieval house. Together they formed the formal approach to the seventeenth century house

THE MIDDLE COURT

The Middle Court was the forecourt of the seventeenth century house and has recently been restored. It is laid out in a very simple but formal manner with two plain grass 'greens' bordered by gravel paths. Such simple designs using grass and gravel were much favoured by British gardeners in the late seventeenth and early eighteenth centuries.

The highly ornate façade of the Stables' entrance

THE STABLE COURT

The Stable Court lies beyond the Middle Court and forms the outer court of the formal approach to the House. Its layout, consisting of four gravelled 'quarters' bordered by cobbled driveways, was only discovered in 1987 and has had to be restored. The two perimeter walls and gateways have also been rebuilt, for they were demolished, probably in the 1790s, at about the same time as the cobbled 'driveways' and cobbled 'quarters' were covered over, to make way for a new circular drive which swept up to the Edney Gates and across to the stables.

THE STABLES

The Stables were probably built in the 1670s and were evidently designed to reflect the splendour of the house, on which they are clearly modelled. The only significant differences between the two buildings are the bonding of the brick (the house is English, the stables Flemish), the massive pediment (seen in the picture left), which may well be a later addition, designed to break up the great length of the building, and the decorative treatment of the façade. The most distinctive feature of the stable façade is the series of Ionic pilasters intended to express the building's use by mirroring the heel posts dividing each horse stall. Such sophisticated treatment of a stable façade was highly unusual in the seventeenth century but not unique, for the 'new' stables erected at Warwick Castle in 1667 (but demolished in 1765) displayed very similar features and both buildings may well have been designed by the same hand, Roger or William Hurlbutt.

EDNEY GATES

The Edney Gates were made and erected between 1714 and 1718 for John Morgan, then owner of Tredegar, by the brothers William and Simon Edney, gatesmiths of Bristol, and are a fine example of early eighteenth century decorative wrought ironwork. William Edney was undoubtedly the most important gatesmith to have worked in the West Country in the eighteenth century. Payment for the gates and railings is recorded in the set of annual accounts kept by James Pratt, agent to the Tredegar Estate from 1701-1732; their total cost then amounted to over a thousand pounds

GARDENS

The overall plan of the gardens is Tudor in origin. The gardens then consisted of five walled enclosures located to the south west of the house. In the early 1700s this layout was apparently changed and the walls realigned and reconstructed in brick to make just three walled enclosures, linked by one central gravel path which ran central to the house. This is the layout that survives today. The largest of these enclosures contains the orchard, the Head Gardener's cottage, the Agent's office and other ancillary garden buildings and offices. The remaining two enclosures, now known as the Orangery and Cedar Gardens, were directly overlooked by the ground and first floor state rooms and were laid out in a very formal geometrical manner with parterres of coloured gravel and grass, bordered by low cut box hedges enclosing flower beds, all punctuated with clipped trees of box, holly or yew. This type of garden was very fashionable around 1700, particularly in Holland.

THE ORANGERY GARDEN

The Orangery Garden is being restored to something like its original early eighteenth century appearance, based on the evidence of a recent archaeological survey.

The Orangery Garden

Below left: The Head Gardener's Cottage

The Orangery

In this garden, fruits, such as apples, pears, peaches and cherries, would have been grown, the trees horizontally trained or *espaliered* against the high brick walls. The stone tiles which project from just below the tops of the walls would have helped to protect the blossom and fruit from frosts and cold winds. In the warmer summer months, less hardy fruit trees such as orange and lemon trees and other tender plants, would have been taken out of the Orangery and arranged in a formal pattern around the garden, the trees still in their pots.

THE CEDAR GARDEN

In the late eighteenth century and in Victorian times the gardens were largely redesigned and replanted. Octavius Morgan thought that it was probably Mr. Walker, Head Gardener from 1782-1801, who changed everything and who *'planted the gardens with all the new trees and shrubs which had at that time been recently introduced from America.'*

In the 1930s a sunken garden was laid out between the house and the lake. The original design incorporated a series of herbaceous borders and rose beds, divided by box hedging and flagged pathways and overlooked by an ornamental Italian *tempietta*. This garden has recently been restored, using many of the species that are known to have been part of the original planting scheme.

THE ORANGERY

The Orangery was erected in the early 1700s at about the same time as the garden walls and was added to the rear of the stables. Orangeries were essentially conservatories or greenhouses designed to conserve during the harsh winter months exotic fruits and tender *greens* such as orange and lemon trees, aloes, bays, myrtles and oleanders.

In the Cedar Garden there is a memorial erected to Sir Briggs, the horse that carried Captain Godfrey Morgan, later Viscount Tredegar, at the Charge of the Light Brigade in 1854

33

THE PARK

An early print of Tredegar

The Lake in winter

The park surrounding the house was one of the foremost designed landscapes in Wales. By the eighteenth century it covered over a thousand acres and its boundaries are clearly defined on a map prepared for Thomas Morgan c.1770 by Robert Snell.

Dominating the park were a series of formal avenues of oak, walnut and chestnut trees, the most prominent being the great double avenue which climbed up to the Gaer, an iron-age hill fort. They were planted in the early 1700s and symbolised the authority of the Morgan family.

In 1790 the family employed a landscape gardener, Adam Mickle, to landscape the park and give it a more natural aspect. Mickle's original scheme included not only the creation of an artificial lake, *the Great Pool*, but also envisaged the demolition of the Stables, the Edney Gates, the Stable and Middle Courts, the Walled Garden, the Orangery and most of the formal avenues. His aim was to create a vast expanse of grass, sweeping right up to the house and across to the lake, giving an uninterrupted view of the house in a *natural* parkland setting. Fortunately, only part of

'Building the Lake' 1791

Mickle's suggested scheme was adopted and the Stables, the Edney Gates, the Walled Gardens, the Orangery and one avenue survive.

In Victorian times, Mickle's great sweep of open ground between the house and the lake was partly obscured by the planting of ornamental conifers and rhododendrons, while in the twentieth century the landscape beyond has been obliterated by urban development. Adam Mickle and the Morgans themselves unwittingly laid the foundations for this creeping urbanisation by allowing the construction of the Newport to Cardiff toll road (the A48) which Mickle supervised in 1790. This effectively divided the park in two. Nevertheless, Mickle made a great effort to hide the road by constructing a high wall, which he, in turn, concealed behind an equally high grass bank in an attempt to preserve the magnificent vista along the one remaining formal avenue. Sadly, the motorway planners of the twentieth century failed to demonstrate the same concern. The grass bank was removed when the A48 was realigned to make way for the construction of the M4 motorway.

THE HOME FARM

Like many country estates Tredegar was very much a self-sufficient community with its own Home Farm providing the family and their staff with most of the goods and services they required. The farm buildings are clustered close to the rear service entrance of the house and range in date from the early seventeenth to the twentieth centuries.

THE BREWHOUSE

The Brewhouse, located near the rear service entrance of the house, may originally have been the stables for the medieval house. However, for the last two hundred years or so, the building was used for brewing beer and only ceased production early this century. Adjoining it was the Bakehouse, which, unfortunately, was demolished in the 1970s, but the huge ovens have been preserved and can be viewed from the Brewhouse courtyard.

THE GREATER AND LESSER BARNS

Across the main cobbled yard is the Greater Barn and, beyond the large double gates to the right, the Lesser Barn. At one time these two buildings formed one enormous barn over 255 feet in length but the central section was destroyed by fire in the middle of the nineteenth century. These barns were not only used for the storage of grain and hay; they also housed the estate fire engine, a snow plough, a game cart for bringing game back from the shoots, a covered wagon for the use of the servants, and a stick house in which a *stick man* was employed to chop wood for the house fires.

BRYAN'S BUILDING

Opposite the Lesser Barn is Bryan's Building, which was named after a Mr. Bryan who was Estate Steward in the early eighteenth century. The building provided accommodation for the Head Gardener and apprentice gardeners and also housed the home farm and agent's offices. Directly in front of Bryan's Building is a weigh bridge, used for weighing farm produce.

VISITORS' CENTRE

The long, low building at right angles to the Lesser Barn, was formerly the Cattle Byre. It has recently been restored and currently houses the Visitors' Centre.

CRAFT WORKSHOPS

The main car park is the site of the Estate Cricket Ground, Bowling Green and Tennis Courts, which were overlooked by a series of open-fronted implement sheds, used for the storage of farm machinery. These have now been enclosed and converted for use as craft workshops.

THE MILL

Behind the Lesser Barn is the Mill which was originally powered by water pumped from the lake via an underground reen. Much of the machinery is still *in situ* but the mill wheel itself no longer survives.

Below and above left: two floral details from carvings in the Brown Room

THE MORGAN FAMILY

Rachel Morgan (1697-1780)

William Morgan (1700-1731)

The earliest recorded owner of a house at Tredegar is Llywelyn ap Morgan who was living here in 1402, but unfortunately he was forced to forfeit his estates as a punishment for supporting the rebellion of Owain Glyndwr. However, later in the fifteenth century, Llywelyn's descendants appear to have recovered Tredegar, and by the end of the century Tredegar was held by one Sir John ap Morgan, who had supported Henry Tudor's successful attempt to gain the English Crown in 1485. He was duly rewarded by being appointed Sheriff of the Lordship of Wentloog, Steward of the Machen Commote and Constable of Newport Castle, and used these positions of power to increase the family's landed wealth. They now had both the motivation and the means for rebuilding Tredegar and this is exactly what the Morgans appear to have done, for the oldest surviving part of the house, the south-west wing, dates from approximately the same period, the late fifteenth or early sixteenth century.

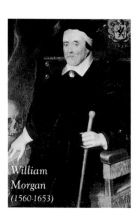

William Morgan (1560-1653)

Elizabeth Morgan (1615-1666)

A NEW TREDEGAR

Although a substantial and impressive building, the medieval house was not going to satisfy the needs and tastes of the Morgan family indefinitely. Hence, soon after the Civil War, between 1664 and 1672, Tredegar was remodelled on an unusually grand scale. William Morgan certainly had the means to rebuild Tredegar, for in 1661 he had married Blanche Morgan, the only daughter of Judge William Morgan of Therrew, King's Attorney for South Wales and a very wealthy man. Her dowry may well have helped to finance the rebuilding of Tredegar and the theory seems to be supported by heraldic evidence. The last quartering of the coat of arms above the main entrance door is believed to relate to the Morgans of Therrew. Thus, by the early 1670s, the Morgans had rebuilt their house on

a very splendid scale. Tredegar, with its lavish interiors, must then have been the architectural wonder of South Wales, a symbol of the Morgan family's wealth and power. For the next 250 years or so they were to be a dominant influence on the political, social and economic life of the counties of Brecon, Glamorgan and Monmouth.

THE GOOD LIFE

In 1715 the family's wealth was considerably enhanced when John Morgan of Tredegar inherited the valuable estate of his unmarried uncle. His son, William Morgan, who succeeded in 1719, clearly intended to live life to the full. In 1721 he paid £61. 2s. 11d. for a great silver punchbowl and the following year there are payments for building a racecourse at Cardiff and a cockpit at Newport. In 1724 he married Lady Rachel Cavendish, daughter of the 2nd Duke of Devonshire, and it was probably no coincidence that, in the following year, William was created a Knight of the Bath. Unfortunately, he was unable to fulfil all his personal and family ambitions for in 1731 he died, aged only thirty.

Lady Rachel, his young widow, lived for another fifty years, jealously guarding the interests of her four children. When her only son died, unmarried, in 1763, she fought unsuccessfully against her brother-in-law, Thomas Morgan, for nineteen years in the Court of Chancery, to gain the estate for her surviving daughter. Curiously, Thomas's three sons also all died unmarried and in 1792 the estates passed to their sister, Jane. Fortunately, however, the family name was retained, for her husband, Sir Charles Gould, was granted the name and arms of Morgan by Royal licence.

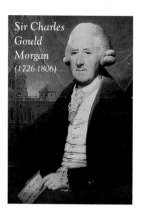

Sir Charles Gould Morgan (1726-1806)

ENTREPRENEURS

Sir Charles Gould (1726–1806) had married Jane Morgan in 1758 and had pursued a very successful legal career culminating in his appointment as Judge Advocate General in 1771. On acceding to the